GRETA MAGNUSSON GROSSMAN

Modern Design
from Sweden to California

Harriet Harriss | Naomi House

LUND
HUMPHRIES

First published in 2021 by Lund Humphries
in association with R & Company

Lund Humphries
Office 3, Book House
261A City Road
London EC1V 1JX
UK

www.lundhumphries.com

Greta Magnusson Grossman:
Modern Design from Sweden to California
© Harriet Harriss and Naomi House, 2021
All rights reserved

ISBN: 978–1–84822–357–8

A Cataloguing-in-Publication record for this book is
available from the British Library.

Front cover: Interior of the Magnusson Grossman
House, Waynecrest Drive, Beverly Hills, 1948–49
Photo: Julius Schulman (courtesy of the Greta
Magnusson Grossman design records and papers
located at R & Company, New York)

Copy edited by Pamela Bertram
Designed by Jacqui Cornish
Proofread by Patrick Cole
Cover designed by Adrian Hunt
Set in Circular Std
Printed in China

The publisher and the authors gratefully acknowledge
the support of R & Company Gallery, New York, USA.

We would like to give special thanks and credit to
Mina Warchavchik Hugerth of R & Company for her
role as Editorial Advisor of the Work.

The publisher and the authors gratefully acknowledge
the support of GUBI A/S, Copenhagen, Denmark.

GUBI

Contents

Foreword

STUREGATAN TO SUNSET: GRETA MAGNUSSON GROSSMAN AND THE IMMIGRATION OF STYLE

In 1996, I visited an older woman in the San Diego suburb of Encinitas on a tip from a realtor who had recently sold a house built by the then little-known architect and designer Greta Magnusson Grossman. That turned out to be her last known address, and the woman I met that day had been a friend of Magnusson Grossman's for nearly thirty years, after the two met at a painting club at the local community center. She described Magnusson Grossman as a fierce person with an intense personality and a great sense of humor, who liked to paint and drink glögg.[1] To my surprise, the long-time friend had no idea that Magnusson Grossman had previously been an architect and award-winning designer for four decades, nor that she had helped shape what we know today as California modernism or California design.

California, and Los Angeles in particular, was a hotbed of activity and invention throughout the 1920s, 1930s and 1940s, when an influx of thinkers, artists, architects, writers and poets began arriving from Europe to start new lives in the region. These emigres brought new ideas and influences of modernism from the Bauhaus, De Stijl, and beyond. The avant-garde took hold in Southern California, which many perceived as a clean slate full of opportunity, open spaces, low costs of living, moderate temperatures, and adventurous communities.

Magnusson Grossman arrived in San Francisco in the summer of 1940 by way of a Japanese ocean liner and was almost immediately offered a job in Los Angeles, where she moved to with her husband, Billy Grossman. Within a year, Magnusson Grossman had opened a small storefront on Rodeo Drive that advertised modern design from Scandinavia. The American space was called Studio, the name she

had also given to her Stockholm store that had also had a prestigious address. Located on Sturegatan, a famous street in the Östermalm district of central Stockholm, it was just a few blocks from upscale waterfront hotels and Kungliga Operan (the Royal Swedish Opera). On Rodeo Drive, Magnusson Grossman's neighbor was Paul László, the Hungarian emigre architect and designer with a celebrity clientele, and it did not take long for Magnusson Grossman to find her place among the social scene of the Los Angeles elite.

Around 1946, Magnusson Grossman was offered the very prominent job of heading the modern design floor of Barker Brothers, the self-proclaimed largest department store in the world at the time. One of the most prominent interiors that Magnusson Grossman created during this period was the Trousdale House, published on the cover of *House Beautiful* in 1949; it featured almost entirely her designs and reflected a sober refinement. In a design proposal for Frank Sinatra from the same time, we again see many of Magnusson Grossman's creations filling the elegant room (which was sadly never realised but can be seen in an original sketch housed at the R & Company Archives). While at Barker Brothers, Magnusson Grossman was introduced to dozens of manufacturers, including Ralph O. Smith, who made her now-iconic line of table and floor lamps by hand. Eventually, Magnusson Grossman forged her relationships with those manufacturers, which led to license agreements for her unique designs.

Magnusson Grossman subsequently set up her own architectural practice and design business out of the first home she designed for herself at the top of Coldwater Canyon. When she began construction on the house in 1945, it was the first

Design drawing for the Sinatra residence interior. Greta Magnusson Grossman design records and papers.
Located in the R & Company Archives, New York, NY

one on the hill and commanded an extraordinary view of all of LA. The 'simple brown house'[2] hung deftly over a cliff, with walls of glass from floor to ceiling as if Magnusson Grossman was metaphorically conquering this new territory. Built with a massive stone fireplace and stone floor in the living room (the only elements that survive from the original design), it was an architectural marvel. It also served as her office and allowed her and Billy to work from home.

Combining *funkis* (Swedish 'functional' modernism) and 'California cool', Magnusson Grossman's particular brand of modernism has stood the test of time. Nearly twenty-five years since her death, her designs have finally become iconic, and she is now considered one of the most important female designers of her era. Although much is still to be discovered about her work, the renewed interest and appreciation for Magnusson Grossman's contributions in otherwise male-dominated fields have grown tremendously and begun to change our distorted views of history. With great enthusiasm, I witness the research and study of her career become the focus for a new generation of design historians and museum curators. In this book, Harriet Harriss and Naomi House continue this trend and explore a deeper understanding of the woman who immigrated her own sense of style while designing remarkable spaces. As we learn more about her life and career, Magnusson Grossman has, at last, earned her spot in the history of modern design.

Evan Snyderman

Acknowledgements

The authors wish to thank: Jacob Gubi, for choosing to remanufacture some of Magnusson Grossman's most iconic pieces and for his generosity in supporting the production of this book; Michelle Jackson-Beckett, Evan Snyderman, and Mina Warchavchik Hugerth of R & Company in New York, whose rigorous and faithful dedication toward archiving American mid-century modernism has afforded Magnusson Grossman's work the comprehensive visual catalogue it deserves, and that so many design libraries and acclaimed academic archives have failed to achieve; and additionally Evan Snyderman, for his thoughtful and thought-provoking written accounts of Magnusson Grossman that encouraged us to look at Magnusson Grossman's work through a lens of our own choosing. There are also two key texts, and by implication two vitally important authors, upon which this book has depended enormously: Andrea Codrington, author of *Greta Magnusson Grossman – A Car and Some Shorts* (2010); and Lily Kane, author of an exhibition catalogue entitled *Greta Magnusson Grossman: Designer* (2000), whose copy held at the Victoria & Albert Museum in London has its pages coming loose, due to our repeated visits.

Further to this, we would like to thank our Commissioning Editor (Architecture and Design), Val Rose at Lund Humphries, our Anglo-Swedish friend and colleague, Monika Parrinder, for her outstanding critique of our early drafts and editorial support, photographer Fredric Boukari in Sweden, Viviane El Kmati and Yara Feghali of Folly Feast Lab in LA, and finally, the readers of this text, for their curiosity and their willingness to hear a different kind of story and a different way of telling it.

This book is dedicated to the many women designers who have, as a consequence of pervasive and persistent gender inequality, been relegated to obscurity. We will find you, in time.

Introduction: Towards a Gender-Critical Design History

Harriet Harriss | Naomi House

'Modern furniture is a growth, progressing out of the needs of contemporary living, Mrs. Grossman points out. "It is not a superimposed style, but an answer to present conditions. That is why it is! It has developed out of our own preferences for living in a modern way . . ."'

Rose Henderson, interview with Greta Magnusson Grossman (1951)[1]

How architecture is written about, who is written about and by whom has become a pressing concern within architectural discourse. The methodological approach underpinning this book seeks to do two things: first, to give an account of the overlooked, misattributed, misappropriated and largely ignored contribution of one significant designer, whose experience is not atypical; and second, to explore a methodology as to how women designers can be written about differently. To do this effectively, we need to confront the core assumptions upon which the canon of architectural knowledge and understanding is based and question how we capture, contextualise, analyse and synthesise a designer's contribution.

Greta Magnusson Grossman (Fig.1) was a prolific designer working within the male-dominated world of mid-century modern design, whose status and influence has been largely ignored. She was the ultimate polymath – an industrial designer, interior designer and architect working within two fascinating contexts: Scandinavia and North America. Beginning by setting out Magnusson Grossman's background, education and the formative years of her career in Sweden, the book describes how she and her husband, the British jazz

musician and band leader Billy Grossman, moved to Los Angeles in 1940. It then discusses the studio they opened on Rodeo Drive and the avant-garde LA community in which the Magnusson Grossmans operated. Her Swedish functionalist approach to interior design was an instant hit in Los Angeles and she soon attracted celebrity clients, including Greta Garbo, Ingrid Bergman, Joan Fontaine, Gracie Allen and Frank Sinatra. Magnusson Grossman additionally designed at least fourteen homes in Los Angeles, one in San Francisco and one back in her native Sweden, not to mention many more in partnership with other architects. Of these, at least ten are still thought to be standing, although many have been substantially altered. Finally, the book explores Magnusson Grossman's contemporary impact, including the relaunch of her lighting and furniture and her influence on today's designers.

Magnusson Grossman is largely remembered today for her work as a furniture and lighting designer, but her practice as an interior designer and architect has been almost entirely overlooked by academic records. This book catalogues and emphasises the significance of her contribution to the canon of interior design, making the connections between ideas she tested at the scale of the product to those she pioneered at the scale of the interior environment.

As female designers and co-authors, we have failed to find ourselves adequately reflected among those who have been designated 'masters' of the discipline and practice, making it necessary to look inside the fundamentals of architecture and interior design through a gender-critical, feminist lens. Previously in our co-authored scholarship,

1   Portrait of Greta Magnusson Grossman, 1959.
Photograph by Julius Shulman

seems that despite her impressive back catalogue of LA work in particular, Magnusson Grossman's legacy as a designer and architect has either been appropriated by others, or misattributed to her white, male peers.

Throughout this book we have chosen, after some debate, to identify Greta Magnusson Grossman as 'Magnusson Grossman'. Writer and curator Lily Kane, who spent many years investigating Magnusson Grossman, notes in her essay (published in *Greta Magnusson Grossman: Designer*, the catalogue for the 2000 exhibition of Magnusson Grossman's work at R 20th Century, now R & Company, in New York) that she opted 'to refer to her as Grossman, rather than Magnusson Grossman, despite the Scandinavian tradition for women to be known by both their family name and their married name', 'for the sake of ease'.[4] However, we have decided that Magnusson Grossman's dual heritage is highly relevant to our narrative and that citing both her family name and married name throughout the text underpins her Swedish-American identity. It was her identity of choice: the name she chose for her business cards. We have also noticed throughout our research that Magnusson Grossman's Swedish heritage is emphasised in the numerous journal articles that illustrate her career between c.1930 and 1960, yet for two-thirds of this time she was a resident of California. Perhaps her Swedish origins appealed to the design press at the time – certainly they attributed a degree of exoticism to her and, by default, her work. That she was also married to an Anglo-Jewish jazz band leader somewhat adds to this construction of her identity as *other*, making her highly marketable in an industry that was increasingly dependent on a favourable media to promote and sell its wares.

Our initial task is to write Greta Magnusson Grossman back into the canon of design history, in particular that of modernism – easily the most significant cultural, political and social movement of the 20th century. However, this task is made more problematic because modernism itself has an uneasy relationship with marginal discourses. In Jane Jacobs' seminal work, *The Death and Life of Great American Cities*, the urban activist challenges modern architecture's 'functional segregation' that frames a 'split between domestic and public life'.[5]

we have asserted that the practice of space-making – in particular the making of the interior – is strategically and fundamentally a feminist action[2] and that we should reclaim the nomenclature of interior design as 'women's work'. We see Magnusson Grossman's interiors as the point of convergence for all aspects of her work, providing the crucible through which the different design objects, spaces and surfaces emerge.

In her essay 'Greta Magnusson Grossman: Walking Away', writer Arianna Schioldager asks, 'why has design pioneer Greta Magnusson Grossman so long remained a footnote in the annals of mid-century modern history, even in the midst of her own revival?'[3] Not only has Magnusson Grossman been largely written out of the history of mid-20th-century design, but the authorship of some of the key architectural works that illustrate her career during the 1950s has also been erased. It

The underlying principles of modernism established a clear distinction between home and work, the private and the public – and there is a discomfort in the non-binary position that is presented by professional women, in particular, who occupy both spheres. Facing discrimination even from the so-called radical institutions that educated them, women were often only welcomed into the more feminine disciplines, such as the textile department of the Bauhaus, for example (where no universal policy existed for the admittance of women to the institution as a whole).[6]

To reinsert Magnusson Grossman into the canon alongside the established and recognised modernist work with which she critically aligns, we must first accept the construction of the canon as it stands. This would mean accepting that the men currently recognised as masters of the discipline(s) are rightly attributed this status and that their work should be the benchmark by which all other work is judged. As feminist writers, we disagree with this and would argue that for history to be rewritten equally, it first needs to be dismantled and reconstructed in its entirety. Where the existing masters might end up in the reshuffle is uncertain.

Instead, we need to assert the integrity of the work, independent of the established canon. Such a project relies implicitly on the activities and writings of the recently formalised decolonisation movement. As journalist Dalia Gebrial argues, 'Such a movement . . . needs to understand its position as responding to live issues of inequality, colonialism and oppression – rather than just being a matter of legacies, or unearthing historical accounts for the sake of it. To do this kind of work . . . is to dig where you have access . . . in the interest of social justice',[7] which accurately captures why we were required to rely almost exclusively upon magazine articles, from trade papers to Sunday supplements, in order to forensically piece together the material needed to construct a life. The exceptions were two catalogue essays – the first, archival, by Andrea Codrington (2010) and the second, by Lily Kane (2000), to accompany an exhibition. They are women writers to whom we owe a debt of gratitude for providing a road map through the various and disparate fragments of evidence.

Of the many ambitions we had for this book, constructing a 'decolonised' lost legacy proved particularly challenging due to the paradoxical problem of using 'colonised' evidence to propose a 'decolonised' model of capture and a new body of evidence. However, the 'decolonial turn'[8] within feminism is necessarily open-ended and contested. The sheer range of the manifestations of colonisation in different parts of the world and the extent to which knowledge frameworks, canons and cultures – and also lands, waters, bodies, identities, emotions and minds – are colonised ensure that decolonising projects will continue to be works in progress.[9] What feminism has gained from postcolonial theory and, in turn, decolonisation, is the understanding that knowledge emerges from within a particular geopolitical, intellectual space or set of experiences. To challenge knowledge is to covet the intersections through which it is trafficked, consumed and understood in different geographies.[10] By experimenting with a fledgling feminist historical restitution methodology, we attempt to confront the gender-biased historical amnesia characteristic of the period in which Magnusson Grossman operated. Given the definition of a 'canon of work' as a list of design objects considered to be permanently established, of the highest quality and accepted as genuine, then what makes an object an icon relies upon the reader's taste more than the historian's accuracy.

Feminism has had a powerful and long-standing influence on the development of architecture and urban design, although this is rarely acknowledged.[11] From this perspective, we must first accept that women's contribution to architecture and interior design has been largely overlooked across the 20th century and that recent political events, including the #Rhodesmustfall and #MeToo movements, have triggered a renewed attempt to redress discriminatory imbalances. This book is, therefore, joining an expanding area in design publishing as increasing numbers of female academics and undergraduate students grow tired of their invisibility and, instead, identify with the protest chant, 'You can't be what you can't see'. Furthermore, while this book will focus most keenly on Magnusson Grossman's interiors, it will illustrate and articulate the intersections, influences and exchanges between her products, furniture, lighting and architecture too. There continues to be a good deal of interest in mid-century modern design – here defined as the architecture, interiors and furniture as well as graphics produced in the period between the early 1930s and the mid-1960s – particularly the Scandinavian and Californian versions, and Magnusson Grossman operated at the intersection of the two in a fascinating way.

Magnusson Grossman's cultural heritage was born out of an ongoing and complex interrelationship between design and aestheticism. Art historian Nils G. Wollin, author of *Modern Swedish Decorative Art* (1931), 'saw Swedish achievements in the "decorative" and "industrial" arts as part of a historical process, leavened by the "characteristically democratic tendencies of the Swedish community"'.[12] The spirit of Swedish design was seen by Wollin to be rooted in its craft traditions, an idea that we explore further in Chapter 1. This craft heritage was also evident in the pedagogy of Sweden's educational institutions, thus shaping Magnusson Grossman's studies and initial work experience in designing and making furniture. She was educated during a time when Swedish design was becoming globally acknowledged, but it was also tempered by significant political moves towards social democracy. In Sweden during the 1920s and 1930s (and later), as elsewhere in Europe, design was appropriated by the state as a tool for social reform – a significant paradigm shift that recognised its political agency – and thus Magnusson Grossman's early career as a designer was shaped by the belief that design had the capacity to improve the everyday lives of ordinary people. Although a common trope of the Modern Movement more broadly, the embedding of this ideology within Swedish culture enabled the rapid proliferation of a social democratic political agenda through the design of the domestic landscape.

Swedish design was much celebrated in the architectural and design press during the 1930s, both in Europe and in the United States. In his 1940 book, *An Introduction to Modern Architecture*, author J.M. Richards describes P. Morton Shand's writing in the *Architectural Review* as 'more responsible than anyone else for the *Review*'s, and therefore for English architects', contact with modern Continental building'.[13] The dissemination of Swedish design within the UK in particular established an appetite for modernism from Scandinavia and its Continental cousins that would

be realised after the Second World War with the birth of the Welfare State. We can only speculate as to the role Magnusson Grossman might have played in this narrative if she and Billy had chosen to relocate to Billy's homeland rather than to the United States in 1940, for here she would have found a small community of emigre architects, designers and intellectuals, many of whom had made their home in the north London suburb of Hampstead and whose pre-war experiments in democratic design were transformed into wholesale solutions during the post-war period. Instead, largely by chance, Magnusson Grossman arrived in Los Angeles shortly after the outbreak of the Second World War in Europe, entering into a world that appeared receptive to newcomers and to the democratic design principles that underpinned her portfolio of work. The narrative that Magnusson Grossman underwent a seamless transition between countries, however, is misleading. Although on the surface her LA career was certainly prolific, she nevertheless remained an outsider, as we will discuss later.

In addition to her foreign status, a *Blueprint* article by Tim Abrahams from 2011 illustrates other biases that Magnusson Grossman – and, consequently, her legacy – have been forced to endure. Abrahams states: 'It is hard to say what hampered Magnusson Grossman most as an architect: sexism, her lack of qualifications or the skills she undoubtedly had in other areas. Ostracised by the male-dominated architectural scene which grew up around the Case Study Houses, Grossman was further compromised by having no formal architectural training.'[14] Although sympathetic to Magnusson Grossman's cause, the implication here is that her absence from the canon of modernism was a matter of lacking an architectural qualification – an astonishing claim considering that world-leading architects including Le Corbusier, Louis Sullivan, Frank Lloyd Wright and Mies van der Rohe had no degree in architecture and yet their credibility as key proponents within the field of modern architecture and design is never called into question as a consequence.[15]

Abrahams continues his investigation by pointing to her physical appearance as a possible cause of her later obscurity: 'Perhaps because she was so glamorous and because her work crossed not just continents and époques but different professional worlds, Magnusson Grossman slipped through the net of history.'[16] Magnusson Grossman herself seems to have been frustrated by the emphasis that the media placed on her gender and her looks. In interviews, she is often at pains to point out that she is as capable as any man of wielding a carpentry tool or securing work, which was at times caricatured on the opposite side of the spectrum while still overstating physical attributes. In an interview Magnusson Grossman gave to *American Artist* in 1951, Rose Henderson comments, 'Her physique is on the rugged side, which is fortunate, as her work requires considerable strength. No craftsman can do the manual work for you, she insists. You have to do it all yourself in order to bring out the spirit of the design and make it an integrated whole . . . "The only advantage a man has in furniture designing is his greater physical strength."'[17] Abrahams' article further states that Magnusson Grossman 'was also hampered by her success as a furniture and interior designer, becoming best known for her work for furniture manufacturer Glenn of California and the department store Barker Brothers . . .',[18] which again reveals a gendered perception of success and capability, considering many of her male peers were instead celebrated as polymaths.

Can we really blame Greta Magnusson Grossman's thwarted architectural legacy on her success in the field of furniture and interiors, as Tim Abrahams suggests? With the rise of the fourth wave of feminism, it seems timely to question this analysis. Rather than simply accept that Magnusson Grossman's legacy as a key figure of both Swedish functionalism and the Los Angeles design scene of the 1940s and 1950s was impacted by her gender, appearance and proclivity for designing largely domestic interiors, we need to unpick this set of circumstances and question the conditions under which Magnusson Grossman's career developed. Abrahams ends his *Blueprint* article by proposing an alternative reading of Magnusson Grossman's legacy. His proposition is that she has been there all along as a 'phantom figure', haunting the iconic images of the period; 'if we were to acquaint ourselves with Grossman's work as an oeuvre and to watch again the Hollywood films of the Fifties and look once more at Julius Shulman's pictures of modernist interiors, we might realise that, in actual fact, we have been familiar with the work of this enigmatic Swede all along.'[19]

The absorption of Magnusson Grossman's work into the background context of what we understand as mid-century modern suggests that we need to pay more attention to the peripheral spaces and objects that shape our perception of it. As such, this book is both an attempt to honour Magnusson Grossman's career and legacy as well as to bring into focus the importance of domestic culture to the wider discourse surrounding histories of architecture and design. In her essay 'Everyday and "Other" Spaces', architecture scholar Mary McLeod questions the place and validity of domestic culture within critical and historical discourse. Whereas many cultural commentators are guilty of marginalising design practices that focus on the domestic interior, others are seen to 'grant' them 'a place in aesthetic culture'.[20] As Magnusson Grossman's architectural contribution was almost exclusively housing-based and by implication domestic – save for a couple of installations – could this be another reason why her work was further dismissed? Could this also explain why attempted acts of restitution to date have been led by curators and manufacturers, as opposed to being led by academics or historians?

In the book *Greta Magnusson Grossman – A Car and Some Shorts: One Architect's Journey from Sweden to Southern California*, R & Company's co-founder and principal, Evan Snyderman, contends that it was the misattribution of Greta's work that provided 'the perfect example of what I thought was wrong in the business', prompting the need to 'take on stewardship of her legacy'.[21] As his interest deepened, he discovered only a few 'scant articles' on her career, despite the many significant milestones. Similarly, the manufacturer Jacob Gubi, CEO and director of the Stockholm-based Gubi furniture and lighting company, has built his business upon discovering forgotten designers such as Barba Corsini, Jacques Adnet, Mathieu Matégot and Robert Dudley Best. These designers are among those whose contributions – through a process of re-engineering and re-release – have launched an industrial assault upon academic omissions. Commercial and curatorial impetus aside, historians now have more to feed on than the carcass of a forgotten career.

The sofa and chair, above left, were designed last year by Greta Magnusson Grossman for Sherman/Bertram of California. The Glenn of California chair at right, styled especially to permit proper sitting posture, won a Good Design Award in 1952.

Still beautiful and still much in demand is this modern version of the kidney-shaped sofa, which Greta Grossman designed in 1937, while still in Stockholm. In 1940, Brown-Saltman purchased the design — the first Mrs. Grossman sold in the United States—and is now manufacturing it with foam rubber construction.

Good Design Is Appearance Plus Comfort

SWEDISH-BORN DESIGNER WORKS TOWARD THE PERFECT COMBINATION

To date, it has been difficult to sell, but the most important point to keep in mind when designing upholstered furniture is the proper posture of the human body.

That is the belief of Designer Greta Magnusson Grossman, who is continually working toward the ideal combination of appearance plus healthful posture and comfort. The major problem in designing a seating piece which is conducive to proper posture — the difficulty in selling it — lies in the fact that such a piece may be unconventional in appearance. And the public buys first for appearance, second for comfort and health features.

"When you can combine appearance and fulfill ideal posture requirements, then you have something," says this attractive young blonde designer.

Facts Known

Certain facts, she points out, are known about good sitting positions. Forty years ago, a German studied this problem and wrote about it; a Swedish doctor brought out a book on the subject in 1947. In America, hardly anything is being done by industry toward attaining the perfect combination, and nearly all research on sitting postures is being taken up by schools.

Most of the so-called "posture chairs" of today are poor in that they violate one of the most important requirements: one should always be able to move about in a chair, to change positions. Mrs. Grossman's latest attempt to combine appearance and comfort was in a chair designed for Glenn of California.

A possible solution to the problem lies in that relatively new and extremely popular material, foam rubber. This product offers the designer the advantage of being able to create light-scale furniture which is comfortable. The currently desired flat effect — rather than the puffy, balloon look — can be attained with foam rubber to create a soft and comfortable seating piece.

For real luxury, Mrs. Grossman cites the combination of coil springs and foam rubber. But, she warns, this is impractical because of cost. "The most extravagant piece I have ever done," she recalls, "was a coil-springed sofa with 4½" foam rubber, covered with down. This was a 28-foot piece, custom made for a Texas oil millionaire." (In most cases Grossman-designed foam rubber pieces utilize No-Sag springs.)

Problems Encountered

All is not perfect in working with foam rubber, however. Even this almost-ideal material has its problems. Foam rubber furniture making is not just a case of laying on a slab of the rubber. There is occasional difficulty in keeping foam rubber flat on a large surface after use. In some (not all) cases, the fabric covering the foam rubber will wrinkle under certain circumstances.

Another problem lies in trying to glue the upholstery to the foam rubber. This is especially difficult when using textured or striped fabrics — which must be kept absolutely straight. The consumer, too, has a problem with foam rubber pieces — ordinary cleaning solvents must not be used on them, as the rubber will deteriorate as a

result. Purchasers should be warned of this fact and told what type of solvent to use, so that they will receive continuous satisfaction from their foam rubber furniture.

In spite of these problems, Mrs. Grossman believes that foam rubber brings wonderful potentials to the designer and she utilizes it in all of her custom work, as well as in some of her manufactured lines. In these latter, the difficulties mentioned above sometimes push the price too high for practicability, she says.

However, Sherman/Bertram of California, one of the firms for which Mrs. Grossman is designing, now manufactures not only the standard-construction upholstered pieces, but an increasing amount of foam rubber work. Martin Brattrud, of Gardena, executes

her designs in foam rubber exclusively. And a sofa which she designed for Brown-Saltman in 1940 — her first piece for any American manufacturer — which has been selling well, ever since that time, is currently being produced with foam rubber.

Studied in Sweden

Mrs. Grossman received design and architectural training in Sweden, where she operated her own upholstering and retail shop. She was well known in other countries — as she is rapidly becoming famous here — and her work was delivered from Stockholm as far as Panama, Poland, England, and France.

Her first stop in the United States in 1940 (she was on her way to New York) was at San Francisco's Market Week. There she became acquainted with the late Dave Saltman, of Brown-Saltman, who purchased the sofa design now converted to foam rubber. Greta Grossman was so impressed with California upon her arrival that it was not until 1947 that she reached New York, her original destination — and then she was in the eastern city only temporarily.

Instead, in 1940, she came to southern California, where she opened a retail shop on Rodeo Drive in Beverly Hills, featuring light, modern furniture. People streamed into her shop to see and admire the advanced styles (which included wrought iron work), but few

(to page 16)

Martin Brattrud, manufacturing foam rubber constructions exclusively, executed the above chair, design for which was created by Greta Grossman in 1949.

Another foam rubber piece by Martin Brattrud is the Grossman sofa above. Mrs. Grossman designed the tables for Glenn of California.

GRETA MAGNUSSON GROSSMAN

6   April, 1953 | Western Upholstery Furniture & Bedding   7

2   Kidney-shaped sofa, 1937. 'Good Design Is Appearance Plus Comfort: Swedish-born Designer Works Toward the Perfect Combination', *Western Upholstery Furniture & Bedding*, April 1953

Within feminist discourse, women's complicity in their plight is a difficult subject to discuss. The reasons why Magnusson Grossman chose to leave LA at the height of her career are a subject of speculation explored later in the book. That her stepdaughter resisted Evan Snyderman's request to access her archive for some six years only serves to fuel a sense of intrigue,[22] while simultaneously affirming the lack of willingness on the part of women to acknowledge each other's achievements, if at all our own. Design is no different to wider society insofar as women's work is often undervalued or overlooked entirely. Any concerted discussion concerning the influence and impact of Magnusson Grossman's work inevitably has to contend with the murky world of misattribution identified by Snyderman, as well as the repeated copying of her work over time. However, Magnusson Grossman was not just an inventor; she was also an innovator, able to absorb and aggregate ideas drawn from multiple sources in many of her designs and herself, blurring the boundary between inspiration and appropriation.

In the example of her kidney-shaped sofa (Fig.2), designed in Sweden in 1937 and bought by Brown-Saltman Furniture in 1940 (just after Magnusson Grossman arrived in California),[23] she was evidently influenced by similar sofa styles that were ubiquitous within this period. This iteration, intentional or otherwise, highlights the problem of authorship within the arena of mass-produced design. At the same time, how can we measure the impact that Magnusson Grossman's version had on later creations? What further complicates an accurate assessment of Magnusson Grossman's influence is the need to recognise how much less successful future designers might have been without her work as an exemplar.

To describe our motivation for writing about Magnusson Grossman as solely a matter of historical, restitutional justice would be disingenuous. Greta Magnusson Grossman was a truly great designer, regardless of how this greatness was, or was not, captured and acknowledged. Her work is worthy of a compendium of works, with or without the additional contextual analysis that this book offers. As Schioldager describes it in her 2013 *Art Papers* article, 'even in celebratory retrospective, Greta Grossman remains an unremembered great, a pioneering figure invisible amongst the visible curves of her spindle-back lounge chair and the slender lines of her Grasshopper lamp'.[24] The writer goes on to describe Magnusson Grossman's ability to rescale a room through the clever use of colour,[25] her skill in elevating the status of ordinary materials,[26] and her ability to work 'with a characteristic rhythm of elastic interpretation, unbound by those who came before'.[27] Subsequently, this book is obliged to strike a balance between offering what the feminist philosopher

Rosi Braidotti might describe as a 'tentative' methodology for feminist historical restitution and a selective catalogue of the work itself.

The book is organised into four sections. The first offers a chronological overview of Greta Magnusson Grossman's education and early career in Sweden, contextualising this within the framework of wider cultural and political events of the time. The second chapter moves to California, exploring the development of Magnusson Grossman's career as an architect and interior designer. The third and fourth chapters return to the fundamental themes of the narrative, re-situating Magnusson Grossman's work within an understanding of interior design practice in particular, as well as beginning to rebuild her legacy within the canon of modernism and beyond. Here we acknowledge Magnusson Grossman's capacity to cross disciplines, working within a range of modes. More importantly, we emphasise that her work is best understood through her interiors as the place where these practices converge. What this book shows is that Magnusson Grossman's outputs are central rather than peripheral to the canon of 20th-century architecture and design, and that the value of her work needs to be examined in order for it to be better recognised and understood.

3   Portrait of Greta Magnusson Grossman, California, 1943

1   Swedish Origins

'Women have traditionally been associated with the interior, with the detailed and the fragmentary.'

Carmen Espegel (2018)[1]

'By striving for beauty at the same time as observing the need for utility, the woman not only satisfies a legitimate desire in her own nature but also exerts a profound influence on the other members in the home of which she is the soul . . .'

Ellen Key (1899)[2]

Greta Magnusson Grossman (Fig.3) was born in Helsingborg, Sweden, on 21 July 1906. Helsingborg is a coastal city in the south of the country within touching distance of Denmark, 10 km across the Öresund Strait. Andrea Codrington, the author of the most comprehensive biographical essay on Greta Magnusson Grossman, describes Helsingborg as 'a town that has had the unique task over the centuries of both staving off and absorbing all things foreign'.[3] Magnusson Grossman's geographical origins seem to operate as a touchstone for her later migration from Sweden to the US – certainly, her life and career would be framed around both her Swedish design sensibility and its translation into an alien context. Furthermore, Magnusson Grossman was born into a world which was on the cusp of immense disruption and change, and her willingness to embrace modernity in all its guises is evident in both the life choices that she made as well as in the objects and spaces that she designed.

ARTISTIC ORIGINS

Magnusson Grossman's family history suggests a readymade connection to the world of Swedish design and craft. Her parents, Thilda and Johan, seem to have been progressive in their outlook and ambitions for their only daughter, whose artistic proclivity was encouraged alongside what Codrington describes as her 'less than feminine'[4] pursuits. Magnusson Grossman's paternal grandfather was a builder who built the house she grew up in. In an interview Magnusson Grossman gave with *House & Garden* magazine in 1947 she states, 'I have wood in my soul',[5] and her cousin, Anne-Marie Bohlin, remembers sculpture being Greta's main 'preoccupation'.[6] Whether or not we choose to believe that artistic talent is hereditary, Magnusson Grossman's academic record testifies to her abilities in this area, and the highest mark in her pre-university exams was for drawing.

After attending Ebba Lundberg's *högre läroverk för flickor* [high school for girls] until 1927, which offered a comprehensive all-round education similar to that offered to boys at the time, Magnusson Grossman did a woodworking apprenticeship at local furniture manufacturer Kärnans. Codrington draws our attention to the gendered nature of this environment, which was fundamentally male, leading many cultural commentators of the time to reflect on Magnusson Grossman's propensity for manual labour. A 1933 article points out that during the apprenticeship at Kärnans, she was taught 'how to handle a saw and a plane with the same strength as almost all her male colleagues'.[7] Not content with the skills she was learning during the day, Magnusson Grossman additionally enrolled in evening classes at a local trade school where she learnt technical drawing. It was during this period that her interest in furniture design really began to develop, and although Magnusson Grossman would remain passionate about fine art throughout her life, her career began to shift towards industrial design.

PEDAGOGICAL INFLUENCES AND PARALLEL CONTEXTS

Sweden in the 1920s and 1930s was a country receptive to the role of design in underpinning the principles of a democratic society. In 1920, art historian Gregor Paulsson became the director of Svenska Slöjdföreningen [Swedish Society of Crafts and Design], from 1976 named Svensk Form. The organisation had been founded in 1845 and facilitated 'intermediary work between artists and industry'[8] — much like the more well-known Deutscher Werkbund [German Labour League], established in Munich in 1907 for artists, architects, designers and industrialists. Enriching the possibilities of what design could be and do, the Svenska Institutet för Standarder [Swedish Institute for Standards] was formed in 1922, setting manufacturing standards across construction, healthcare and product design. These guidelines would have an influence on the need for all designers to address the utility of designed objects in both the home and the workplace.

By 1923, when the Gothenburg Exhibition (Fig.4) opened its gates to the public and marked the 300th anniversary of the founding of the city, Sweden was ready to present itself as a modern country, albeit most buildings in the exhibition followed classical architectural principles. The products displayed likewise largely represented the elite of Swedish applied arts rather than the everyday goods promoted by Svensk Form, but there was nonetheless, a growing national interest in the accessibility and affordability of 'good design'.

Magnusson Grossman's ambition to pursue her growing passion for furniture and industrial design resulted in the decision to move to Stockholm to attend the Högre Konstindustriella Skolan [Higher School of Industrial Art], later known as Konstfack, which was largely considered the pre-eminent art and design school in Stockholm. Konstfack had been teaching furniture design since 1899, but it had not been a hugely popular choice of subject until 1928, the year Magnusson Grossman enrolled there with a scholarship. There were seven students in her year group — a significant increase over previous years. Author Sigrid Ekland Nyström suggests that this came about because there was 'an increased public interest in interior design, support from Stockholm's Chamber of Commerce and the concerted publicity efforts of Svenska Slöjdföreningen'[9] [Svensk Form]. Certainly, the timing was right for a cultural shift towards the design and

4 Gothenburg Exhibition, 1923

manufacture of everyday goods that might enrich the lives of the ordinary Swedish family.

Despite specialising in furniture, Magnusson Grossman's education was broad. While a student she was exposed to ceramics, metalwork and textiles, as well as life drawing, decorative painting, ornamental sculpting and art history.[10] She studied with two other women, Margareta Köhler and Britta Wetter, which was especially unusual as there had only ever been two previous female graduates: Märta Larsson-Skyllings, who went on to work for architect and furniture designer Carl Malmsten (a devotee of traditional Swedish craftsmanship), and Märta Måås-Fjetterström, who designed textiles for furniture and interiors.[11] In a 1933 interview Magnusson Grossman asks, 'Why shouldn't a woman be able to become a furniture designer? . . . Throughout time it was she who created the home – a tradition as good as any to build on.'[12] This recognition of the place of the home within Swedish culture, and more broadly within narratives of design, would come to inform both the public consciousness as well as Magnusson Grossman's own burgeoning career.

Konstfack offered a fundamentally traditional education, but it was inflected with a new concern for the philosophies expounded by modernist thinkers in mainland Europe. In Sweden, modernism was construed as interchangeable with 'functionalism', or *funkis* as it was referred to colloquially. One of Magnusson Grossman's classmates, Ralph Alton, described what was produced at this time as 'a little bit Malmsten, a little bit Stockholmsutställningen'.[13] Here he was referencing Carl Malmsten – who opposed functionalism – and the Stockholm Exhibition held in 1930 which would have a great influence on funkis.

The 1920s had seen a tension between traditionalism and modernism, not just in Sweden but across Europe – and the admiration for Swedish design in the UK, for example, was still largely for expensive handmade objects rather than design for industry.[14]

The 1923 Stockholm City Hall, designed by Ragnar Östberg, is symbolic of the conflicts permeating Swedish design during this time (Fig.5). Design historian Gillian Naylor suggests that the building represents 'the apotheosis of Sweden's National Romanticism, as well as civic pride in

5   The inauguration of Stockholm City Hall by Ragnar Östberg, 1923

craftsmanship'.[15] She continues, 'The building rose . . . from the surrounding huddle of workshops, as a vindication of the viability (and the sophistication) of the craft ideal. According to F.R. Yerbury, (writing in 1925), it was, "perhaps the finest building in the world . . .".'[16]

Gunnar Asplund's 1928 Stockholm Public Library (Fig.6) is another key structure of this period which reflects how Swedes aimed to combine folk traditions, classicism and modernity. The pure symmetrical forms of Asplund's design are translated into the Swedish vernacular using brick and 'conceived, in the teeth of bitter opposition, as a showpiece for Paulsson's desire to further democratise Swedish design and architecture'.[17]

While Magnusson Grossman continued her education, the Deutscher Werkbund provided the accepted framework for design reform throughout Europe. Hermann Muthesius, the founder of the Werkbund, in a critique of Arts and Crafts design, stated, 'The curse that lies upon their [British] products . . . is one of economic impossibility.'[18] For

6   Stockholm Public Library by Gunnar Asplund, 1928

Muthesius, the spirit of the age was characterised by the rational rather than the creative, celebrating intellectual endeavour in place of intuitive response. Where the Arts and Crafts Movement focused on the authenticity of materials and the role of the craftsman in generating appropriate design for everyday use, Muthesius' philosophy found higher meaning in the universality of form.[19] As previously discussed, Svensk Form shared a similar worldview.

The Deutscher Werkbund's philosophical positions and continental influence were especially evident in the Weissenhofsiedlung buildings at their 1927 exhibition in Stuttgart. Here, proponents of the Modern Movement active across Europe put together a showcase of prototype dwellings for workers. Intended to exemplify the principles of the movement, the exhibition included twenty-one examples of modernist housing designed by a number of its key protagonists, including Le Corbusier, Walter Gropius and J.J.P. Oud. Mies van der Rohe oversaw the project, commissioning the architects and supervising the building construction. However, although intended as prototype houses for workers, none of the buildings erected tested standardised housing components or worked with an appropriate budget, thus

inadvertently highlighting the shortcomings of their ambitions.

Another significant event in terms of establishing modernism across Europe was the 1925 Paris World's Fair – Exposition Internationale des Arts Décoratifs et Industriels Modernes [International Exhibition of Modern Decorative and Industrial Arts] – which looked to bring together examples of *Style Moderne* (later termed Art Deco), including architecture, interior design and furniture, as well as glass and other decorative arts from across Europe and around the world. Although only nineteen years old when this exhibition took place, perhaps for Magnusson Grossman – a fledgling designer and maker – the most influential exhibit would have been Le Corbusier's Pavillon de L'Esprit Nouveau (Fig.7), the French pavilion for the journal *L'Esprit Nouveau* that had been founded in 1920 by Le Corbusier and Amédée Ozenfant to promote Purism and attack the excessive decoration of architecture. The pavilion stood out among the more obviously traditional structures at the exhibition and, as Le Corbusier commented in a statement at the time, 'Our pavilion will contain only standard things created by industry in factories and mass-produced, truly the objects of today.'[20] This emphasis on the design and manufacture of ordinary things would prove to be hugely significant within the growing discourse surrounding modernism and its socio-political stance.

The Swedish exhibit in Paris was curated by Gregor Paulsson and the pavilion was designed by Carl Bergsten, complete with a range of living room furniture for the Swedish department store, Nordiska Kompaniet, colloquially known as NK. Uno Åhrén, in a critique of the exhibit, says, 'that the chair and table and bed should have such difficulty finding modern designs is because people have not realised that they are also apparatuses'.[21] However, elsewhere the Swedish contribution to the Paris Exposition was more highly regarded. P. Morton Shand, writing for the *Architectural Review*, praised the pavilion, suggesting that it was 'perfectly edited'.[22] Morton Shand was instrumental in digesting Sweden's contribution to the new language of design for a British audience, thus ensuring the dissemination of Swedish design beyond its borders. From the perspective of UK-based architectural scholars, it is no coincidence that the British appetite for Swedish modernism reflected a national inclination toward coveting and adopting designs that were symbolically, if not practically, more meritocratic.

THE 'TOTAL WORK OF ART'

The broad and diverse education that Magnusson Grossman received at Konstfack was not uncommon during this early period of the 20th century. The Bauhaus, in Weimar, Germany, had opened in 1919, offering an education that combined crafts with fine art along the principles of the *gesamtkunstwerk* (the 'total work of art'). Although not offering architecture until its move to Dessau in 1927, the idea of the 'total work of art' was embedded in Bauhaus philosophy, which contended that the practice of art and design (including architecture) should accommodate all disciplines – a practitioner, whether sculptor or textile designer, painter or architect, should have experience of both adjacent and seemingly 'other' ways of working. In the UK, the Royal College of Art, an institution founded in 1837 as the Government School of Design, enrolled students onto a diverse array of programmes that by the 1930s, and into the 1940s, included industrial design, graphic design and fashion – as well as the more traditional courses that had started life based around the philosophies of the Arts and Crafts Movement. Here, too, the overlap between disciplines was actively encouraged, as well as a

7   Pavillon de l'Esprit Nouveau by Le Corbusier and Pierre Jeanneret, 1925

new emphasis on modern design practices. It was also the context in which the two authors of this book met – as colleagues – and by implication informs our ease with, and recognition of, inter- and trans-disciplinary practices.

In Sweden, KTH, Kungliga Tekniska Högskolan [Royal Institute of Technology], was founded in 1846 as a Sunday School of Drawing and transformed into the School of Technology in 1878, reflecting a developing concern for the design of everyday things. By 1912, the school had made technical drawing compulsory for all of those studying, and in 1915 it introduced furniture design as an independent discipline. Within fifteen years, these furniture specialists had become so key to the construction of the Swedish welfare state that they had begun to call themselves 'furniture architects' – thus appropriating the term 'architecture' as a verb rather than simply as a noun. Within all of these institutions, the diverse combination of craft practices, industrial design and architecture converge and, as we will argue later in the book, the place where they converge is within the *interior*. Certainly, Greta Magnusson Grossman's capacity for designing and making across this spectrum can be most readily seen in her construction of interior environments.

FUNKIS

'How easy it has been for some time to use originality to draw attention to oneself – but what we need now is the ability to efface ourselves.'

Uno Åhrén (1925)[23]

In his recently published examination of the history of Swedish design, design historian Lasse Brunnström explores the origins of functionalism within Sweden's heritage of craft and industry. Unlike earlier historians of Swedish design, including Penny Sparke and Jonathan Woodham, whom Brunnström cites as being guilty of locating the origins of Swedish design within the milieu of handicrafts,[24] Brunnström contends that, although in architecture elements of the new functionalism were critiqued as 'un-Swedish', 'much of the

functionalist message was deeply rooted . . . in Swedish building traditions'.[25] Brunnström goes on to quote art history professor Ingeborg Glambek, who suggests that Swedish architecture and design in the 1920s '"was perceived as something completely special, as an original and creative mix of old Swedish tradition and modern innovation" by foreign observers'.[26] J.M. Richards, in his 1940 book *An Introduction to Modern Architecture*, exemplifies this more nuanced position. For Richards, the modernist 'puritas' of the Bauhaus was 'modified, in Sweden particularly, by a strong craft tradition. A preference for natural materials gave the Swedish brand of modern architecture a more human character which appealed strongly to those who preferred the break with the past to be softened by a charm of manner generally only associated with period reminiscence.'[27]

Magnusson Grossman's launch as a professional designer, after completing her studies at Konstfack and winning a travel scholarship to Europe in the summer of 1931, coincided with an increased media interest in the influence of modernism upon Swedish design. At this point, the Swedish press were fascinated by the functionalism of the International Movement and how this aspect of modernist philosophy might be reconciled with a Swedish concern for material comfort. It was widely accepted that Sweden's take on the modernist aesthetic was tempered by its sensibility for timber and colour. Codrington points out: 'When quizzed in one interview as to whether modern furniture could actually provide a pleasurable seating experience, the designer leapt up from an armchair with some amount of exasperation and exclaimed, "Can a *funkis* chair be comfortable! Sit down in that low, blue one and you'll see."'[28] In another article, titled 'Functionalism and Colour', Magnusson Grossman goes further: 'There are some who would say, seeing all this colour – especially the colour of the walls – that it's misaligned with true functionalism . . . But there's also such a thing as the eye's functionalism as well! The colour of walls can make a big room smaller and more intimate or a tiny room bigger, at least when it comes to the question of the impression one gets. That must also be called functionalism.'[29]

We can see here how the essence of traditional Swedish architecture, which looked to maximise light in architecture as well as in the streetscape, was reflected in the innovations of functionalism.[30] What was also of importance to both the Swedish funkis project and more widely to modernism as a whole was that the simplicity of these new living environments might both facilitate the eradication of dirt – and by extension, disease – from the home, while simultaneously morally elevating those who adopted modern ways of living. The funkis home ensured that 'virtue and aesthetics went hand in hand'.[31]

THE STOCKHOLM EXHIBITION

'If the decade that followed the First World War and the 1917 October Revolution was when the "unfinished modern project" first acquired its avant-gardist character, Stockholm 1930 was the moment when this cultural rupture was rendered as a socially acceptable synthesis, one which by 1944 had been developed into the Swedish Welfare State . . .'

Kenneth Frampton (2008)[32]

'The most awkward and also true thing that can be said about the 1930 exhibition is that it was not Swedish.'

Sydsvenska Dagbladet (1930)[33]

'The world will look up to Sweden . . . as the supreme exponent of Modernism which has succeeded in finding its own soul and embellishing itself with a purely mechanistic grace.'

P. Morton Shand (1930)[34]

The Stockholm Exhibition of 1930 – organised jointly by the city of Stockholm and Svensk Form under the directorship of Gregor Paulsson and with Gunnar Asplund as chief architect – served to embed the idea of funkis within contemporary Swedish design and industry (Fig.8). The undisputed influencer of the 1951 Festival of Britain, the Stockholm Exhibition set the tone for a version of modernism free from the weight of concrete and tubular steel. With its emphasis on the use of natural materials, in particular timber, the focal point of the exhibition was the 260-foot (80 metres)

8   Stockholm Exhibition, 1930. Photograph by Gustaf W. Cronquist

tall 'Social Democrat' advertising tower. According to architectural historian Nicholas Bullock, in his review of Eva Rudberg's *The Stockholm Exhibition 1930: Modernism's Breakthrough in Swedish Architecture*, this was 'modern architecture in holiday mood',[35] a comment that rather overlooks the fact that the design on display was anything but frivolous, but rather a serious engagement with the complexities of modern living.

Although it was well received internationally, the Stockholm Exhibition was widely critiqued within Sweden. Malmsten was deeply concerned that the architecture and design that the exhibition promoted were unsuitable for Swedish homes.[36] He saw 'the rationalisation of the home according to functionalist principles a debasement of its traditional role as an intimate place for gathering and repose'.[37] Criticism from such a respected source did not go uncontested and, in 1931, the exhibition organisers, Svensk Form (at that time still called Svenska Slöjdföreningen), issued a manifesto, *acceptera* (accept), as a counter-response to Malmsten's position. *acceptera* 'stressed the role of art: "The new architecture needs the help of free art. Painting and sculpture must emerge more strongly within architecture's framework. Not, however, as subservient 'decorative' design . . . But as free, independent design."'[38] As Codrington says, 'The document was intended as an encouraging call to arms for Swedish designers and architects to take the latest Continental currents and adapt them in distinctly local ways.'[39] *acceptera* demanded the rejection of what its authors perceived as old-fashioned design principles and aesthetics that refused to embrace the needs of a wider community.

As with the Swedish Pavilion at the 1925 Paris Exposition, British architectural critic and journalist P. Morton Shand was very supportive of the Stockholm Exhibition, giving it a number of favourable write-ups in the British press and coining the phrase 'Swedish Grace' in the *Architectural Review* of August 1930, which over time has become assimilated into common terminology and provides a descriptor for Swedish modernism that distinguishes it from its more extreme versions visible elsewhere in Europe at this time. Naylor, in her essay 'Swedish Grace', explores this edition of the *Architectural Review* alongside another

contemporaneous text by Nils G. Wollin titled *Modern Swedish Decorative Art*, published in 1931. For Morton Shand, states Naylor, the Stockholm Exhibition represented a paradigm shift within Swedish design, cutting its links with the past and proposing a form of modernism that he saw as more achievable than those proposed by the European avant-garde. Deliberately ignoring Russian Constructivism as an obvious influence, the critic believed that 'these buildings represent the revitalisation of Swedish grace'.[40]

Controversial now, Morton Shand seems to have been drawn to the idea that Sweden's version of modernism was born out of an uncontaminated tradition, evident in 'the purity of her racial stock'.[41] This conflation of Swedish modernism with racial purity certainly problematises the moral foundations of funkis. Even if this quotation reveals Morton Shand's own political position rather than the fundamental principles of Swedish functionalism, he was not alone in drawing out the underlying link between Swedish national identity and the origins of good design.

The Stockholm Exhibition received four million visitors, all of whom were invited to view everything from factory products such as 'stackable pots from AGA' and 'curtain fabrics designed by Greta Galn' to 'simple tableware by Hald and Kåge'.[42] This was an event that looked to represent every Swedish citizen. Paulsson's vision for the exhibition was 'that the purposeful represented beauty, held true for the radicals. Mass production needed simple shapes and smooth surfaces that were easy to clean. Small houses needed cheap, space-saving and comfortable standard furniture. The home's interior design had to become a utility design, it should be practical and rational like in the workplace.'[43]

Drawing inspiration from the Deutscher Werkbund, Paulsson's curatorial approach emphasised the need for collaboration between arts and industry. Reflecting on the Stockholm Exhibition, Richards provides a detailed overview of its significance:

> Previously modern buildings had been seen only in the form of isolated structures that inevitably looked stranger than they really were when surrounded by the mixed architectural styles of the average city street, but at Stockholm a whole

sequence of buildings – as might be a whole new quarter of a town – were designed and laid out in a consistently modern style, and the public, walking among them, was given a first glimpse of modern architecture not as a new fashion in design but as a newly conceived environment.[44]

For many in Sweden, the Stockholm Exhibition embodied a shift towards a concern for the design of the whole urban landscape, not simply for the manufacture of its disparate parts. What is more, for the first time, architects and designers were able to recognise the importance of their role in the construction of this utopia.

HOME AND THE EVERYDAY

In 1919, eleven years before the Stockholm Exhibition, Gregor Paulsson, the key figure in the development of Svensk Form and author of *Vackrare Vardagsvara* [*More Beautiful Everyday Goods* – variously translated as *Better Things for Everyday Life* or *Beautiful Everyday Ware*] (Fig.9), had supported the merging of art and industry, 'Allowing applied artists . . . to sit making trinkets for an interested and affluent few while the form of industrial products is determined by purely technical draftsmen can scarcely be considered right.'[45] '[N]ow was the time', said Paulsson, for 'the artist to step in and give the goods a shape . . .' and, 'in the industries, where the design is not obvious, introduce modern beauty'.[46] Paulsson was interested in society as a whole, demanding 'a definite change from the isolated production of individuals to the conscious work of a whole generation for a culture of form on a broad social basis'.[47]

Paulsson's text was very much influenced by William Morris but departs from the Arts and Crafts Movement philosophies 'in his insistence that the factory product was more socially viable than handwork', as Naylor reports.[48] This concern for establishing a real connection between design and industry was underpinned by a genuine belief in the intrinsic value of mass-produced, everyday objects for the home.

The writings of Ellen Key were also significant during this period in shaping how Swedish

9   *Vackrare Vardagsvara* [*Beautiful Everyday Ware*] by Gregor Paulsson, 1919. Photograph courtesy of TL Stockholm Sweden

architects and designers thought about objects and interiors. Key was a feminist and educational theorist whose 1897 essay in a women's magazine, 'Beauty in the Home', was immensely influential upon the emergence of the Swedish welfare state and its central focus on the home. When Key composed her 'manifesto', living standards in Sweden were below that of many other European countries. Directing her writing towards the 'woman of the house',[49] she argued for everyday objects and environments that have utility yet are beautiful: 'Only when there is nothing ugly available for sale, when beautiful things are as inexpensive as ugly ones are now, can beauty for everyone be fully realised.'[50] It is once again apparent that the writings of William Morris had proved influential and this rendering of 'the home as the cradle of a new egalitarian culture'[51] underpinned the political climate in Sweden at this time.

During the early to mid-20th century, the movement for social democracy was gaining ground in Sweden and the election of Social Democrat leader Per Albin Hansson as Prime Minister in 1932 signalled the emergence of a welfare state or Folkhem (literally meaning 'people's home'). In conjunction with this increasing concern for the needs and rights of the common person, a large proportion of the population migrated from the countryside to the city, increasing the demand for housing and establishing a new generation of urban consumers.

In many instances, housing in Sweden in the late 19th and early 20th centuries had continued to be built using traditional methods – albeit with an underlying concrete frame – whereas other typologies such as shops and factories were more readily able to embrace the new processes and materials of modernism. 'Prefabricated wooden dwellings – one-family houses and villas – that grew out of the sawmill industry adopted functionalist design on the outside but often preserved traditional planning.'[52]

In 1931, Borohus, a Swedish house manufacturing company established in the 1920s, released a timber catalogue advertising four designs that illustrate the desirable homes of the period: Granebo – national/romantic style; Söderhaga – classicism; Hollywood – an expensive form of modernism; and Funken – modernist but less pretentious.[53] Each of these options offered a variation on a theme but did little to address the changing housing needs of an increasingly urban population. Nevertheless, these new necessities were beginning to be recognised by the state – if not by private enterprise – and through the instrument of centralised government, housing solutions were developed to manage this rapidly shifting situation.

In 1933, the newly formed Bostadssociala Utredningen [Social Housing Commission] instituted standards for housing that had been proposed at the Stockholm Exhibition and lamellhus – multi-dwelling apartment blocks – began to replace more traditional homes. In 1937, state loans were made available for homemakers, making economic investment in the home more accessible to all, and, in 1938, the government appointed twenty-eight home consultants to advise on 'questions of housework and household planning'.[54]

The 1938 Saltsjöbaden Agreement further advanced the cooperative spirit that pervaded Swedish politics at this time.

Alongside this concern for housing standards and the provision of suitable dwellings for all was a growing interest in the interior and the realisation that the organisation of the home – as well as the design of furniture and everyday products – might have a meaningful impact on the everyday life of the Swedish citizen. The Röhsska Museum in Gothenburg was instrumental in 'propagating good taste', organising a number of exhibitions around the theme Vår Bostad [Our House] between 1937 and 1945. The accompanying literature to Vår Bostad proclaimed: 'the home is first and foremost a social problem, only then an aesthetic problem'.[55] This point of view can be interpreted in two ways: understanding housing as a social problem insofar as people need a place to live, or through an idea largely disseminated by the European avant-garde at the time, who propagated the idea that the home could inform the character and morals of its inhabitants. On the other end of the spectrum, the influential Austrian architect Josef Frank, who had emigrated to Sweden in 1933, wanted to 'free housing from being condemned to always want to be art of reformatory'.[56] Notwithstanding, whether they agreed with one side or the other, Swedish designers generally saw the home as the embodiment of their national identity.

While the politics during this period focused, primarily, on the larger social agenda of design and found itself at the centre of ethical debates, the furniture industry remained 'relatively small-scale'[57] and free from ideological deadlocks. There was, however, a growing demand for furniture designers who might provide the industry with solutions to the problem of furnishing the smaller apartments that were springing up in Sweden's towns and cities. There were also moves to find appropriate aesthetic forms for new home technologies such as the telephone and radio.

The gap between the grand narrative of social reform and the practicalities of designing and making furniture and appliances that facilitated the more flexible domestic arrangements demanded by a new urban class needed to be addressed. Responding to the idea of the new modern citizen, NK developed the revolutionary concept of the flat-pack, producing furniture under the name Triva-Bygg. Although flat-pack furniture would later become the core of IKEA's business plan in the 1950s, in the 1930s, Swedish citizens were not yet ready for such innovation. Furniture for the home needed to adapt to a range of conditions, but consumers remained somewhat conservative and the path to win them over was not entirely clear.

The KF – Kooperativa Förbundet [Swedish Cooperative Union] – was active from 1899 as an economic association of consumer-owned companies, but it wasn't until the 1930s that a guild of self-employed interior architects and furniture designers was established. Strangely, Svensk Form seems to have been rather unsupportive of this professionalisation of designers, preferring to highlight the role of 'building' architects in constructing interior environments[58] – a position that appears to favour the idea of the 'total work of art' but simultaneously marginalises the role of the interior and furniture architect.

In 1944, Svensk Form had joined with Kooperativa Förbundet and others with the overarching aim of drawing the public gaze towards the design of the home, encouraging a more flexible approach to the inhabitation and organisation of domestic space.[59] In the same year the HFI – Hemmens Forskningsinstitut (Home Research Institute) – was formed. Funded by the state, it was tasked with investigating 'the nature and status of women's work in the home'.[60] At the same time SAR – Svenska Arkitekters Riksförbund [Swedish Architects' Association] – also carried out studies into the home, although these were largely ergonomic and aimed at the standardisation of furniture and the home itself. Throughout this period, the home operated as the core of Swedish identity and as the focus of design interest. Yet it was also a gendered space and, as such, framed the identity of the new modern woman.

A MODERN WOMAN

After returning from a trip to Stuttgart and Vienna in 1931 funded by a travel grant,[61] the proto-modernist Magnusson Grossman took her portfolio to Axel Einar Hjorth who ran the furniture department at NK near Kungsträdgården. The meeting did not go well: in an interview she gave in the 1980s, Magnusson Grossman stated that she was told that 'they didn't have any facilities for women'.[62] After that, she was briefly employed at the AB Harald Westerberg furniture store on Kungsgatan in Stockholm, but soon quit and formed a partnership with her Konstfack colleague, Erik Ullrich, to establish Studio in April 1933 (Fig.10), designing and making furniture and home accessories. The place soon became a focal point for emerging designers, hosting parties and talks by like-minded professionals, and the partners developed a multinational client base (Plate 2).

Magnusson Grossman eventually developed a partnership with Hjorth at NK as well, designing bespoke furniture for a cosmopolitan audience across Europe and beyond. Hjorth apparently seemed content to collaborate with Magnusson Grossman, if not to employ her directly, after their shared involvement in an exhibition staged by Ludvig Nobel in 1936. That she ended up working with the people who had previously turned her away must have seemed somewhat ironic to Magnusson Grossman at the time, but she was becoming astute at making sound business decisions.

Although the early 1930s was a period of economic recession, the business of interior design in Stockholm appeared buoyant and Magnusson Grossman was quickly picked up by the press across the political spectrum – in particular, the popular liberal newspaper *Aftonbladet* and its conservative counter-balance, *Nya Dagligt Allehanda*, which heralded her as 'our first female furniture architect in action'.[63] In a short time she became 'a poster girl for modern style'[64] and was not alone in her design endeavours, as Stockholm rapidly developed a reputation for funkis design. In 1934, Magnusson Grossman's Konstfack classmate Margareta Köhler joined with artist Marie-Louise Idestam-Blomberg to set up the studio and boutique, Futurum. It seems from these examples that designing for the home had become a productive space of employment.

1933 was a busy year for Magnusson Grossman. She won second prize in the 'combination furniture' category of a furniture competition sponsored by the Stockholm Hantverksföreningen [Stockholm Craft Association][65] – the first woman to win

10   Images of Greta Magnusson Grossman and Erik Ullrich's Studio shop, Stockholm

anything in this competition. She also married Billy Grossman, who played drums at the Tony Grand Hotel and Galerie Moderne, a restaurant and exhibition space inside Dramaten (Sweden's National Theatre in Stockholm), where Konstfack students sometimes exhibited. Grossman was eight years older than Greta and had been integral to Stockholm's jazz scene since the mid-1920s when he had left England to tour Sweden with band leader Dick de Pauw and his Royal Dance Orchestra. This wasn't Billy's first marriage – he was a divorcee with a young daughter – and Stockholm at this time must have seemed 'an attractive place to start over'.[66]

For Magnusson Grossman, life could not be more exciting – just after they were married she won a travel grant from Svensk Form and the newlyweds went abroad together.

There are no records of this trip, but there are a number of articles because Magnusson Grossman wrote for *Nya Dagligt Allehanda* while on the road. The couple travelled to England, France, Switzerland, Italy, Germany and Austria, and Magnusson Grossman contributed to the 'Women and Home' section of the newspaper, 'keeping an eye out for what was new and notable in the world of interior design and architecture'.[67] She wrote a 'Letter from Paris' about the exhibition of contemporary French decorative art at the Grand Palais that depicted a *funkisbarnkammare* [functionalist nursery] using tubular steel. From Milan, she described the interiors of Motta, a bar/restaurant/pasticceria in the Galleria Vittoria Emanuele II, which 'displays the best new Italian furniture, textiles and decoration'.[68] Motta was a focal point for Milan's design scene, designed by Melchiorre Bega and with paintings by Gio Ponti (Fig.11). We can surmise that while there, Magnusson Grossman met and shared ideas with both Ponti and Bega – certainly we know that her work was published in *Domus*, the design magazine founded by Ponti in 1928.

These 'letters' from her travels articulate a perspective of Europe at a time of seismic shift. Adolf Hitler was appointed Chancellor of Germany at the beginning of 1933 and, when Paul von Hindenburg died the following year, he assumed overarching control of both the Chancellery and the Presidency – with a national referendum in August 1934 confirming him as Führer. In Italy, the fascist government of Benito Mussolini that had inspired Hitler was firmly established. In both these countries, architecture and design were utilised to facilitate and promote the ideological position of their leader.

The rumblings of fascist politics would have been visible to Magnusson Grossman during her travels, but the articles she submitted largely focus on her experiences of architecture and design, independent of the political contexts that shaped them. And yet, although Magnusson Grossman's travelogues focus entirely on the task in hand, acting as a cultural commentator and recording her experiences of architecture and design, we can discern from one article written while she travelled through Germany and Austria that she wasn't entirely ignorant of the political manoeuvres of the National Socialists. Here, Magnusson Grossman makes reference to Ramersdorf, an exhibition of thirty-seven houses designed to illustrate 'how one will live according to the emerging principles of the Third Reich'.[69] Aesthetically, these homes, with their 'steep-gabled, retro-historical gingerbread aesthetic'[70] were a long way from the pure functionalism of the Deutscher Werkbund's Weissenhof estate.

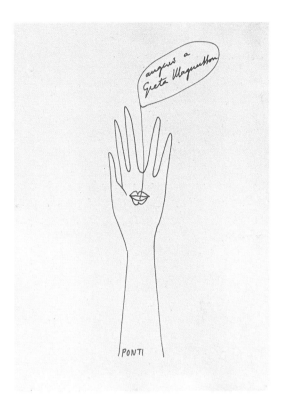

11   Personal note to Magnusson Grossman drawn by Gio Ponti, 1940s

Returning to Sweden in the mid-1930s, the couple resumed their glamorous life, moving into Storskärsgatan 5 in Gärdet, an up-and-coming neighbourhood comprising new lamellar apartment blocks. The Gärdet apartment was open-plan, with a kitchen and bedroom and views of the city beyond (Fig.12 and Plate 1). Between 1935 and 1936, the Magnusson Grossmans were interviewed by a number of different newspapers, revealing a home life centred around domestic activities such as cooking, as well as artistic endeavours including weaving and sculpture. It seems that Magnusson Grossman's role as a travel correspondent for *Nya Dagligt Allehanda* had introduced her to a wider public audience whose interest in design was easily matched by their interest in her as a symbol of modern living. These articles depict an almost utopian fantasy of a couple who appear to embody the zeitgeist. Interviews with the Magnusson

Vid detta arbetsbord ritar fru Grossman sina möbler.

Den inlåsta skatten skulle man kunna säga om Billy Grossmans barskåp, det låses nämligen med kedja och hänglås.

Bland kastruller, stekpannor och hundra attiraljer trollar fru Grossman fram delikata middagar.

Mat och mycken mat och mat i rättan tid

Vad lägger ni mest an på? har vi frågat heminredningsexperten fru Greta Magnusson-Grossman, maka till kapellmästare Billy Grossman.

Jag hade tänkt mig att få tala möbler och idel möbler, när jag häromdagen besökte fru Greta Magnusson-Grossman hemma hos sig i sin trevliga våning på Gärdet. Fru Grossman sköter heminredningsfirman Studio som är hennes liv och själ. Men i stället får jag stifta bekantskap med allt annat än möbler och möbelarkitektur.

»Vad lägger fru Grossman mest an på hemma i sitt eget hem?»

»Ja, det är en hel del det», svarar Greta Grossman och skakar sitt svarta lockiga hår. »Först och främst är det

Husets trevliga brashörna.

En lugn stund vid frukostbordet före dagens id på olika håll.

mat och mycken mat och mat i rättan tid. Inga kotletter och sådana där lättvindiga saker hemma hos mig, nej, rediga långkok tycker jag om att styra med. Stekar och sådant som till exempel gås, stekt så där härligt knaprig, det är det bästa jag vet.»

Det är inte utan att det vattnas i munnen av blotta beskrivningen, men så är också fru Grossman en livlig varelse, som har ett suggererande och medryckande sätt att meddela sig med folk.

Hennes intresse är inte bara mat! Hon både väver och skulpterar på lediga stunder. Hur kan man hinna med så mycket? Maken, kapellmästare Billy Grossman förklarar som svar på den frågan, att han faktiskt har en tusen (Forts. å sid. 42

konstnär till hustru, så mycket hinner hon med. Inte bara affären och sitt yrke som hon ideligen söker förkovra sig och skaffa sig nya lärdomar i, praktiskt och teoretiskt, utan också hemmet får hennes intresse. »Hushållet sköter hon idealiskt

Grossmans highlight a lifestyle where healthy outdoor activities undertaken at weekends are complemented by the interior environments that they inhabit. Indeed, the reports are especially interested in the ways in which the design of the couple's domestic interior frames their private lives. Magnusson Grossman created a scrapbook of press clippings (now in the care of R & Company), in which these articles – in yellowed paper, sometimes with handwritten dates and notes – depict a world that is both thrilling and chic.

A TURNING POINT?

In May 1935, Magnusson Grossman participated in an exhibition at Galerie Moderne, the art salon inside Dramaten, that included work by a number of prominent female designers from the period, including textile designer Åsa Lindström, ceramicist Lisbet Jobs and book designer Ingrid Fogelmarck, all curated into the domestic scene.[71] Although well received, one critic reported 'that it was hardly the *vacker vardagsvara*, or "beautiful everyday ware," that Sweden's famous functionalists had in mind when they penned *acceptera*'.[72] Rather, 'It represents an exclusive, interesting, admirable kind of handicraft, but is a long way off any kind of design for the masses.'[73] Another critic dismissed the work as inferior to that of Svenskt Tenn, the store and workshop opened by design entrepreneur Estrid Ericson in 1924 and the design home to Josef Frank. Perhaps because much of the work on display was designed and made by women, it was all too easy to undermine its intentions. Certainly, describing it as 'handicraft' – and therefore as amateur – does little to validate the collaborative efforts of the participants.

Despite such negative critique, Magnusson Grossman's design career continued to develop and in 1936, she collaborated with Båstad, a spa and health resort that represented the combination of nature and culture that was fashionable at the time. The resort hotel was developed by Ludvig Nobel, a Swedish-Russian engineer and businessman and elder brother of Alfred Nobel, founder of the Nobel Prize. Nobel was very interested in design and interiors and decided to put together an exhibition housed in a renovated grain store. This

13   Interior from the Nobel apartment, 1937

was an early example of 'adaptive re-use', where the original features of the industrial building provided an effective backdrop to a new kind of occupation, offsetting the designed objects on display. Magnusson Grossman was invited to take part, along with Carl Malmsten and the furniture workshop of NK, and her exhibits proved so popular that Nobel's son and his wife invited her to design the interiors of their home (Fig.13 and Plate 3).

The Swedish royal family were also known to have visited the Båstad exhibition and, perhaps buoyed by this commission, Magnusson Grossman decided to design a cradle in honour of the birth of Princess Birgitta in January 1937. Working with textile designer Astrid Sohlman, Magnusson Grossman crafted an object that combined white beech, woven cellophane and embroidered, quilted silk.[74] She exhibited the cradle at the exhibition *Nyttokonst* ['useful art'] in 1937 at the National Museum in Stockholm (Fig.14). Although the

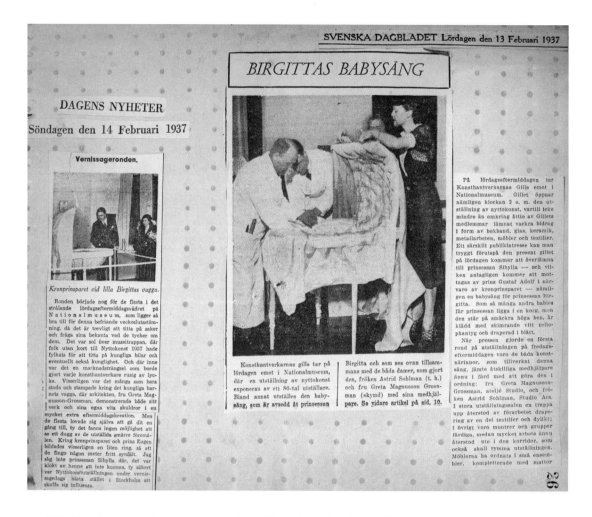

14   Spread from Magnusson Grossman's own scrapbook with articles on the exhibition *Nyttokonst* at the National Museum in Stockholm, 1937

work of eighty designers was displayed, the crib proved to be the most popular exhibit, drawing the attention of the royal family, the public and the press who seem to have been wise to Magnusson Grossman's deft handling of the publicity. 'Princess Birgitta's fine bed main attraction at exhibition', was the headline in the morning newspaper, *Stockholms-Tidningen*[75] – and saved in Greta's scrapbook. There also appears to have been some discomfort amongst the press regarding Magnusson Grossman's apparent delight in her royal success. *Dagens Nyheter* noted that, while showing the royal family around the exhibition, Magnusson Grossman was 'displaying both her work and her own white shoulders in an extra special tea frock'.[76]

In May 1938, Magnusson Grossman opened a one-woman show at Galerie Moderne (Fig.15). The exhibition consisted of eight domestic room settings that provided a showcase for Magnusson Grossman's particular brand of Swedish functionalism to great effect. The furniture on display was especially vibrant, demonstrating her love of bright, cheerful colours and patterns that embodied a kind of homeliness that was missing from the furniture and interiors of the European avant-garde. As skilled hosts, the Magnusson Grossmans also staged an exhibition opening that would have made it to the society pages of a contemporary magazine. With Billy's Orkester performing and Greta facilitating the proceedings, the evening must have been a great success. The exhibition was reviewed in all of the major national newspapers, reflecting Sweden's ongoing concern for the design of the public realm and, in particular, the need for 'good design' within the home as an illustration of funkis in action. What is apparent is that the press were as important in the transmission of good design as the state – and in the promotion of modern ideas, perhaps they were more successful in communicating the desirability of the modernist dream.

In 1939, Magnusson Grossman enrolled as a part-time student at KTH, recognising that, if she wanted to develop her career further, she would need professionally recognised architectural skills in order to complement her existing 'toolkit'. It is highly likely that while attending the institute Magnusson Grossman would have been taught by Gunnar Asplund – as well as other significant proponents of Swedish modernism who were teaching there at the time – thus exposing her to ideas and opportunities that would have otherwise passed her by.

The key focus of architectural thinking during this period – and certainly across design education – was collective housing and how to organise this new type of interior. Already in 1933, Svensk Form and HSB, the cooperative association for housing, had staged the exhibition *Bostad och Färg* [*Home and Colour*] of two contrasting domestic interiors: one was a 'horror' apartment 'with heavy "fine" furniture and wallpaper decorated with medallions, and the other an "ideal" apartment with modern furnishings'.[77] The intention of this exhibition was to promote the funkis approach of state-led good design, where the emphasis on colour – including wallpaper and paint colour samples – reminds us how funkis addressed every aspect of the interior.

In 1935, a housing experiment was erected in Stockholm involving a collaboration between Sven Markelius, Alva Myrdal – both prominent architects of functionalism – and the Yrkeskvinnors Klubb

15   Exhibition at the Galerie Moderne with furniture by Studio, 1938

[Professional Women's Club], an organisation that promoted and gave a voice to working women at this time.[78] And in 1936, the Yrkeskvinnors Klubb and Svensk Form decided to put together the exhibition *YK-Huset, Elva familjer visa sina hem* [*Eleven Families Show Their Homes*] to promote recent innovations in the design of the funkis interior. YK-Huset was a collective apartment block in Gärdet, built in 1939 and designed along the principles of the Soviet Social Condenser – a new type of post-Revolutionary architecture with shared amenities including a kindergarten, a restaurant and a gymnasium. What was innovative about this housing, however, was that the primary user was the working mother.[79]

Writing in the exhibition catalogue, Svensk Form member Åke Stavenow characterised its main objectives: 'First, it wants to promote a dwelling model which through its design seems to set a good example and which in its general organisation offers a fortunate solution to the problems which have occurred because more and more married women get employed. Second, it wants to promote interior and furniture design, that presently is flourishing.'[80]

Magnusson Grossman was invited to design an apartment for YK-Huset – a home for a librarian and her three-year-old daughter. The presence of shared amenities meant that the apartments themselves conformed to minimum space standards but were also released from the constraints of designing spaces within which to eat and play. Magnusson Grossman's exhibit represented a shift in focus. Whereas, up until now, she had largely designed furniture and interiors for wealthy clients, here she was able to bring attention to the universality of good design. Here was a designer at the height of her powers – already commercially successful, she was now in the enviable position of being able to test her ideas within the context of the pressing social problems of the day.

AMERICAN DREAMS

In 1939, at the New York World's Fair, the Swedish Pavilion designed by Sven Markelius proved to be a very popular exhibit. Described by Lewis Mumford in the *New Yorker* as 'a miracle of elegant simplicity',[81] the pavilion served to place Swedish functionalism in view of an American audience. Architect and historian Talbot Hamlin described the experience of visiting it as if 'one lives, for a moment, a different kind of life – more ordered, more quiet, more intelligent, less garish'.[82] The catalogue for the Swedish Pavilion outlined its philosophy:

We know the home to be one of the most important factors in modern society. We know

that good homes can be created only by sound people in hygienic houses through education and knowledge with furnishings attuned to the times. We know that beauty and comfort should be provided for all. We know that beauty and high quality can only be achieved through the intimate cooperation of artist and manufacturer. This, in brief, is the meaning of the movement SWEDISH MODERN.[83]

The interiors of the pavilion were undertaken by a number of well-known Swedish designers including Bruno Mathsson, Carl Malmsten, Josef Frank, Axel Larsson and Elias Svedberg, but there was no furniture by women on display. At the same time as the exhibition, the Swedes took advantage of the retail potential by setting up shop in the Rockefeller Center, thus enabling sophisticated New Yorkers to purchase elegant Swedish designs for their own homes.

Although the fair proved that modernism's momentum would only continue to grow, it coincided with the outbreak of the Second World War and Germany's invasion of Poland. Within less than a year, Denmark and Norway had been invaded and occupied. Sweden declared itself 'non-belligerent' but supplied Finland with arms intended to resist Soviet invasion. The country's position additionally prompted thousands of Jews to attempt to flee to Sweden to avoid Nazi persecution, but few felt that conflict could be avoided or that safety could be guaranteed.[84] Billy Grossman's Jewish heritage meant that despite their respective professional success – and in Magnusson Grossman's case, her burgeoning career – remaining in Sweden was potentially dangerous. With this in mind, she and her husband took the difficult decision to abandon everything and leave Europe altogether. Travelling east by air and train across the Soviet Union, they took a boat to Japan and then an ocean liner to San Francisco, arriving in the United States on 27 July 1940.

Plate 1   The Magnusson Grossmans' apartment in Gärdet, 1934. Photograph by Bergne Reklamfoto

Plate 2　Interior from Studio, 1934

above

Plate 4   Barker Brothers Showroom, 1947. Photograph by Harry H. Baskerville, Jr

right

Plate 5   Interior view of a seating area with Cobra shade lamps and furniture by Magnusson Grossman for Barker Brothers. Photograph by Maynard L. Parker

Plate 6   Drop-leaf coffee table in walnut and plastic laminate with wrought iron legs, produced by Glenn of California, 1952

Plate 7   Exterior of the Magnusson Grossman House, Waynecrest Drive,
Beverly Hills, 1948–49. Photograph by Julius Shulman

Plate 8   Interior of the Magnusson Grossman House, Waynecrest Drive, Beverly Hills, 1948–49.
Photograph by Julius Schulman, 1955

Plate 9 Interior of Backus House, Bel Air Estates, Los Angeles, 1949–50.
Photograph by Donald J. Higgins

Plate 10   Exterior of Barham Apartments, Barham Boulevard, Hollywood, Los Angeles, 1950.
Photograph by Donald J. Higgins

Plate 11 Interior of lower structure, Nelson House, Hollywood Knolls, Los Angeles, 1955.
Photograph by John Hartley

Plate 12   Interior view of the living room, Nelson House, Hollywood Knolls, Los Angeles, 1955.
Photograph by John Hartley

Plate 16　Exterior of Hart House, Hollywood Knolls, Los Angeles, 1958.
Photograph by John Hartley

left, top and bottom

Plate 17   Cobra table lamp; and Plate 18   Cobra floor lamp and double-shaded floor lamps, all produced by Ralph O. Smith, 1948–49

below

Plate 19   Grasshopper floor lamp in original colour, produced by Ralph O. Smith, 1947–48

Plate 20   Set of dressers in walnut, designed by Greta Magnusson Grossman for
Glenn of California, Los Angeles, 1952. Photograph by Joe Kramm

Plate 21   Walnut-framed, three-panel room screen with painted wooden balls
on piano wire, produced by Glenn of California, Los Angeles, 1952

2   A Well-Known Designer

'In war periled, dictator encircled Sweden, there is little inclination these days and nights for the syncopated rhythms of swing music. As for the furniture market, there's no demand for anything but sturdy pieces of bomb shelter decor. That's why Mr. and Mrs. Billy Grossman were in San Francisco yesterday, looking forward to new careers in America. He is Scandinavia's pre-war dance band favourite, known as the "Benny Goodman of Sweden." His chic blonde wife, Greta Magnusson Grossman, is a well-known designer of modern furniture. The couple arrived here Saturday aboard the Japanese liner Nakura Maru—she with the number one objective of "buying a car and some shorts" as their first step towards self-Americanization.'

'New Career Sought: Couple Arrive from Sweden', *The San Francisco Examiner*, 29 July 1940[1] (Fig.16)

16   'New Career Sought: Couple Arrive from Sweden', *San Francisco Examiner*, 29 July 1940

As the *San Francisco Examiner* article implies, Magnusson Grossman and her husband were indeed the model emigre couple – educated, cultured, economically productive and self-sufficient – and deemed acceptable in appearance. This propagandist pitch – intended as a warning, as well as a welcome – only served to promote their presence on the LA scene. This became the hallmark of how their world was often captured within the press, which sought to blur the professional and personal aspects of their lives.

RETAIL ON RODEO DRIVE

Although Magnusson Grossman's original intention was to move to New York, which she knew had previously welcomed Swedish design so warmly the year before, the couple soon decided to remain in California. This decision was largely driven by a chance meeting with the businessman and investor David Saltman, whose LA-based company bearing his name had just begun manufacturing a line of modern furniture. The two met during San Francisco's Market Week, an exposition of home furnishings where emergent designers would aim to attract the attention of manufacturers, and during which Saltman bought the rights to manufacture Magnusson Grossman's 1937 kidney-shaped sofa (Fig.2).[2] His portfolio of designers included other recent emigres, such as Paul Frankl and Paul László, and also American designers such as Gilbert Rohde, Henrik Van Keppel and Taylor Green.[3]

Within a matter of months, Magnusson Grossman opened a furniture store on Rodeo Drive (Fig.17), which soon became one of LA's most prestigious shopping districts (László's studio was only two doors away from Magnusson Grossman's). She quickly succeeded in gaining the attention of the local design community, as reflected by the number of articles written about her during this period. The first was in the trade publication *Retailing*, entitled 'Swedish Designer to Work on West Coast', which emphasised Magnusson Grossman's intention to 'devote primary attention to the establishment of her own studio . . . the needs and likes of the individual . . . and furniture, fixtures and rugs . . . to suit the clients [*sic*] taste'.[4] This instinct towards offering bespoke interiors and

stockholm   beverly hills

greta magnusson-grossman, swedish designer,
358 north rodeo drive,
beverly hills, crestview 66624

will be pleased to have you attend the opening of her studio on friday, january 31st, 1941, from 10 a. m. to 6 p. m.

swedish modern furniture, rugs, lamps and other home furnishings.

17   Invitation to Greta Magnusson Grossman's store on Rodeo Drive, Beverly Hills, 31 January 1941

to respond to individual taste shows sensitivity to end-user needs that were atypical of this era – and may, in part at least, account for why Magnusson Grossman attracted so many women as clientele. That she was a working woman – professionally independent and able to generate her own income – is another probable reason. Professional women, regardless of sector or sphere, were in the minority, and so hiring a female designer who reflected their precarious and often marginal position must have held certain appeal.

THE MAKING OF A SWEDISH-AMERICAN

According to the text on her first business card, Magnusson Grossman initially identified herself as a 'Swedish Designer, Stockholm and Beverly Hills locations',[5] asserting her intimacy with Scandinavian design and her role in facilitating the coming together of Swedish and American lifestyles. However, suggesting that she was based in both LA and Stockholm was overly optimistic. With the scale of devastation Europe was left to contend with after the Second World War and the subsequent years of economic depression, it was almost impossible for the majority of migrants and refugees to ever return home. Not surprisingly, Magnusson Grossman's subsequent business cards only refer to her LA practice.

Her identity as an interlocutor of Swedish design within an American context, in contrast, proved more enduring. In a *Los Angeles Times* article entitled 'Home Furnishing Art Ranks High in Sweden', Magnusson Grossman is captured discussing the varying sizes and importance of rooms in the domestic interior and the extent to which 'Sweden is highly conscious of its homes and the manner in which they serve as backgrounds to living.'[6] This was comforting talk that contrasted strongly with other emigres' horror stories from Europe, and no doubt served to cement her appeal to a population looking towards a period of peace and prosperity. Similarly, her November 1941 storefront exhibition at 358 North Rodeo Drive ensured her Swedish origins were conspicuously foregrounded through the selection of decorative elements, catalogued by one reporter as 'hand woven', combining colors into fabrics for rugs, pillows, throws, couch covers and even wraps'.[7]

Within months of arriving in LA, Magnusson Grossman was invited to contribute to an exhibition at Raymond and Raymond, an art gallery in Hollywood – an opportunity that connected her to the wider design community. This continued the following year, 1941, with Magnusson Grossman exhibiting work that was described by one reporter as featuring 'fine clean lines and respect for the inherent beauty of wood and textile'.[8] Having embedded herself within both a community of clients and a community of designers, Magnusson Grossman decided to move her studio from Rodeo Drive in Beverly Hills to a more affordable address on North Highland Avenue in Hollywood. Advertising the move in *Arts and Architecture*, she describes herself as 'a designer of furniture and interiors', notably choosing not to mention her Swedish identity. It is probably safe to assume that, at this moment, Magnusson Grossman either felt sufficiently comfortable with her place in the community to focus on her skills rather than her point of origin as a marketing point, or feared her immigrant status could count against her.

TALENTED WOMEN, UN-WOMANLY AMBITION?

Magnusson Grossman's success has been depicted in many ways, some more explicitly gendered than others. Unlike her male counterparts, her entrepreneurial approach to business was often characterised as an unabashed attachment to self-marketisation. For example, in Codrington's text, *A Car and Some Shorts*, the author states that it was 'Grossman's self-promotional ability and talent [that] garnered positive exposure',[9] identifying her capacity for self-promotion in advance of her skill as a designer, rather than suggesting self-promotion might be a talent in itself. Although it is clear that Codrington is not seeking to diminish Magnusson Grossman's skills as an architect and designer, or indeed to express any distaste at her obvious business acumen, the fact that Magnusson Grossman took full advantage of the marketing opportunities presented via the numerous interviews that she gave to the press both in Sweden and in the US throughout her active career, is important to discuss. Such acumen for self-promotion is evident elsewhere within histories of design and is often perceived as reductive, debasing the practice of design to something driven by commerce rather than ideas and ethics. The designs of Raymond Lowey, for example, are often characterised in this way – the assumption being that his work is very much part of popular culture and therefore lacking the prestige of high art.

Magnusson Grossman's gender further problematises the status of her work. The notion that business acumen is in some way unappealing in women has been much interrogated,[10] but for Magnusson Grossman's male contemporaries to have thrived to the same extent she did would have demanded that they were equally entrepreneurial, and yet this is seldom drawn attention to in historical accounts. When it is mentioned – for example, in Bruce Brooks Pfeiffer's account of architect Max Hoffman, whom he describes as in possession of a 'business acumen bordering on sheer genius'[11] – there is admiration, even though Hoffman and Magnusson Grossman were professionally active during the same period. Pfeiffer and Codrington were writing in 1999 and 2009 respectively, meaning that even contemporary design historians and archivists tend to evaluate women's talents in ways that are different to men. That Magnusson Grossman's appeal and notoriety continued to grow despite this, rather than because of it, is true testimony to the scale of her talent and the extent of her endurance.

In any case, for Magnusson Grossman, design was not just about commercial success or self-promotion. During the Second World War, she attempted to offer her drafting services to help the war effort but was rejected because she was an immigrant. Instead, she volunteered for the Women's Ambulance and Defense Corps, advising on managing blackouts based on her direct experience of them in Stockholm.[12] Consequently, it is hard to square the claim that she solely focused on her own success in light of these acts of discreet civic engagement.

MODERN DESIGN, DESIGNING MODERNISM

As well as appealing to professional, educated women and men, Magnusson Grossman responded to the economics of war in early 1950s America by developing a brand of modernism that struck a balance between, on the one hand, innovative modern furniture and lighting pieces and, on the other, affordable soft furnishings, throws, rugs and plants. She was essentially pioneering a form of interior decorating that is still tremendously popular today. By presenting this juxtaposition as a desirable choice, as

opposed to a financial concession, she did much to inspire consumer confidence. In doing so, she was also inadvertently promoting natural materials, re-use and environmentally sensitive aesthetics.

Magnusson Grossman's design philosophy asserted that design should: respond to the time; encapsulate human factors such as well-being, ergonomics and social interaction; feature natural materials and forms and provide an 'engaging backdrop to a person's activities'.[13] This philosophy was substantially Swedish in origin. What Magnusson Grossman brought was an ability to playfully marry natural forms and materials – such as wood with metal elements – and a keenness for asymmetry. Her ability to amalgamate her European training with the culture of California seems a likely explanation for her success.

Magnusson Grossman's interest in accommodating familiar objects and motifs within the landscape of modern life, translated into her approach to designing interiors. The choice of polished walnut alluded to the integrity of tradition and the vernacular crafts, whereas the asymmetric blending of steel and Formica exalted the industrial ideal within a machine age. Elsewhere, her work was described as offering 'a touch of light and air, of cheerfulness and practicality',[14] but Magnusson Grossman considered her emphasis on comfort, functionality and an elimination of the non-essentials to be a key part of her approach.[15]

THE ORIGINS OF DEMOCRATIC DESIGN

Magnusson Grossman's origins and training positioned her to transpose the Scandinavian principles of 'democratic design' to a new country and context. The ideology from institutions such as Svensk Form, which believed that designs should be affordable for the masses but not stripped of beauty, was a principle that Magnusson Grossman carried on. Adapting these ideals to fit the consumerist culture of the US was no mean feat – although others have analysed the reception of Scandinavian design abroad as a form of mythmaking, as discussed in Chapter 1.[16]

Curiously, democratic design is more often attributed in American design history to Frank Lloyd Wright[17] who looked to establish an 'architecture of democracy' that embodied the nation's zeitgeist. More recently IKEA has claimed it – where the former head designer, Marcus Engman, in an article in *Adweek*, was quoted as saying that IKEA invented the term as recently as 1993.[18] *Forbes* then credited the introduction of democratic design to French designer Philippe Starck in a subsequent article.[19] However, Starck was born in 1949, when Magnusson Grossman's career was already consolidated.

The establishment of Scandinavian design – and consequently a version of democratic design – on the global market, and particularly in the United States, has been attributed to the Lunning Prize. Instituted by Frederik Lunning, agent for the work of Danish designer Georg Jensen in New York, the prize awarded outstanding Scandinavian designers from 1951 to 1970 and was responsible for making Scandinavian design a recognised commodity and for defining its profile.[20] Several historians also point to the Brooklyn Museum's 1954 exhibition, *Design in Scandinavia*, as the official birth of 'Scandinavian design'.[21] Yet this ignores the work that Magnusson Grossman was producing ten years prior to this that encapsulated all of the characteristics of Scandinavian design and was consistently referred to as such by the LA design press during the 1940s.[22]

That Magnusson Grossman helped to develop the profile of both democratic design and Scandinavian design (now often used interchangeably), as well as popularise it, seems clear to us now as we look back at her body of work, but she is not credited with either. Democratic *and* Scandinavian design, by definition, are distinguished as delivering form, function, quality and sustainability at a low price – yet these are principles which Magnusson Grossman embodied at least a decade ahead of *Design in Scandinavia*'s official launch at the Brooklyn Museum exhibition, 30 years ahead of Philippe Stark and half a century ahead of IKEA, making her one of the originators of this approach alongside more well-known protagonists such as the Eames in the US, Isokon in the UK and, of course, Svensk Form in Sweden.

DRESSING THE INTERIOR

Soon after Magnusson Grossman moved to Hollywood in 1943, she was 'discovered' by an executive from Barker Brothers (Fig.18), and her work for the company formed the first major focus of her design activities in the US. Barker Brothers was a home furnishings store in downtown Los Angeles that had become the largest in the world because of its proactive pursuit of home-builders the moment that their construction permits were granted.[23] More importantly, Barker Brothers was a retail store that was catching on to the shift in taste towards modern furniture designs for the home, and Magnusson Grossman's designs for the company were sensitive to her audience.

Magnusson Grossman also designed the Barker Brothers showroom and, in 1947, she was hired as the design consultant to construct an interior 'set' for customers wishing to update their home interiors on a larger scale (Plate 4). This was an innovative move by a company which recognised a gap in the market – no longer were customers simply shopping for single pieces of furniture, they were looking for ideas and advice on how to design their whole home. In an article in *Arts & Architecture*, Barkers Brothers explained its strategy of using 'the talents of a recognised designer' to inspire 'personalized built-in interiors'.[24] At the same time that IKEA in Sweden was beginning to develop its brand, Magnusson Grossman's room-sets for Barker Brothers offered a vision of the modern home that pre-dates IKEA's move into furniture retail and, later, flat-pack. Certainly, IKEA's focus on the showroom as the selling point for an entire fit-out for the home did not take place until the 1950s.

The positive public response to Magnusson Grossman's Barker Brothers designs was further reflected in the decision to dedicate an entire floor of the department store to a 'Modern Shop'. In the Modern Shop, Magnusson Grossman's work was displayed next to that of Alvar Aalto and while all the pieces were – perhaps unsurprisingly – misattributed to him rather than her, they also mistakenly reported his nationality as Swedish rather than Finnish.[25]

Over 6,000 people attended the gala opening of Barker Brothers' Modern Shop and a review of the

ARCHITECTURAL INTERIORS

CUSTOM-BUILT

FOR YOU

GRETA MAGNUSSON GROSSMAN, eminent Swedish designer, is the consultant for this new service at Barkers. It is more than a decorating service. It includes the creation of entire architectural interior backgrounds, specially woven fabrics, specially designed furniture...all under the direction of Mrs. Grossman, whose international experience in all phases of modern design is evinced in all her work. The brilliant rooms, custom designed for Barkers' new Modern Shop, illustrate her sure touch and artistic originality. If you want a highly individual modern home, investigate this service. FIFTH FLOOR

BARKER BROS.
SEVENTH STREET, FLOWER AND FIGUEROA

18   Barker Brothers advertisement featuring Greta Magnusson Grossman's designs, 1947

event featured Magnusson Grossman as one among the 'Up and Coming: Five Whose Stars are Shining in the Design World'[26] (Fig.19). None of the others were women. One of the successful tactics of the Modern Shop was to present a 'domestic landscape' of built-in sofas, tables and cabinets – to essentially set the scene of how the various elements would work together – rather than display them by type. This approach served to highlight Magnusson Grossman's talent for custom-designing space and working across materials and forms. She was invited to create three distinct 'rooms' – a study, a living room and a card room – which she configured using a refined balance of natural tones, wood and her own hand-woven textiles, the latter of which attracted esteem from the media.[27]

Time magazine had described Barker Brothers as the finest example of 'Los Angeles Spirit', which no doubt helped the company to gross

$15.5 million in 1944[28] and presented Magnusson Grossman with 'a distinctly easy entry to first-time customers of modern design'.[29] Astutely, one reporter highlighted, 'Miss [*sic*] Grossman has dispelled many conservative fears over sharply modern . . . by giving enough corners to keep ardent moderns happy but smoothing out many sharp kinks with curves sweeping enough to please the open-minded Victorian.'[30] In *Greta Magnusson Grossman: Designer*, Lily Kane suggests that 'her pieces offered, at first glance, a fairly conservative tone . . . Upon closer look, however, her pieces often revealed unique, even eccentric, touches that allowed the user to have brought Grossman's modernist experimentation with forms into their own homes almost by accident.'[31]

THE CALIFORNIAN DESIGN MOVEMENT

The supply of materials from America's manufacturing industry in the early 1940s was largely unaffected by the war effort, offering a choice of products that enabled Magnusson Grossman to continue the experiments with form, material interface, balance and plasticity that she had begun while still in Sweden. Historians have since characterised the period in which Magnusson Grossman worked as the Californian Design Movement,[32] which largely operated out of Los Angeles between 1945 and 1960. This movement offered young designers and architects a chance to exploit the post-Second World War boom in industrial production and manufacturing in a city dedicated to expansion and technological advancement, often appropriating wartime materials and technologies such as moulded plywood, plastics and industrial steel.

Added to the homegrown community of architects and designers was an influx of European talent, in the form of Second World War refugees and emigres, who brought with them a range of aesthetic influences and, moreover, a desire to experiment with new ideas, materials and concepts. In addition to this, the GI Bill provided servicemen (rather than women, who – although eligible – did not greatly benefit from this initiative) with the opportunity to attend college after returning from

38 YEAR OF DESIGN *continued*

Up and coming

Five whose stars are shining in the design world

Angelo Testa

The meteoric career of this 25-year-old textile designer proves that America is quick to recognize talent that is fresh and inspiration that is different. Testa's bold, often abstract motifs, created in his Chicago studio by the process which he modestly calls "doodling," are in pure, strong color. They support his thesis that prints can make a wall exciting. See one-room apartment, page 30.

Greta Magnusson Grossman

Swedish-born Greta Magnusson Grossman originally planned to be a sculptor. Her feeling for plastic shapes is evident in the furniture, rooms and textiles that she designs and has woven in her California workshop. Her modern, custom-made furniture is a Barker Bros. in Los Angeles. Descended from six generations of house-builders, Mrs. Grossman declares, "I have wood in my soul."

19 'Up and Coming: Five Whose Stars are Shining in the Design World', *House & Garden*, June 1947

the war. California's exemplary state college and university system[33] provided a trained and educated workforce committed to building a more equitable vision of the future, unlike any other being formed elsewhere in the US.

California's tradition of garage-based start-ups, which we often attribute to Bill Gates' creation of Microsoft or Steve Jobs' Apple, far preceded these later iterations and dominated throughout the 1950s. The Eames' home-made Kazam! Machine (named because it transformed thin sheets of wood into complex curved forms as if by magic), allowed them to mass-produce moulded plywood furniture from their apartment. This is an early example of this 'new' tradition – establishing, as early as 1941, an approach to designing and making that highlighted a process of continual testing and modification. The focus on small-scale manufacturing often meant that many designs produced from similar garage-based workshops were limited to the Californian context, due to the cost of shipping items east or internationally. For Magnusson Grossman's work to achieve notoriety beyond the usual constraints facing the Californian small designer-manufacturer, is indicative of her talent and tenacity.

DESIGNING WITH THE PROFESSIONAL WOMAN IN MIND

By the mid-1950s, Magnusson Grossman was designing for either single women or couples without children – couples whose configuration matched her own. Whether this was due to a decision not to have children, or for biological reasons, is not recorded – which is somewhat surprising given the common perception of professional women as bad mothers at the time.[34] Despite not having children, however, Magnusson Grossman designed with 'family cohesion' in mind, arguing that 'Simplicity . . . is the all-important thing in the preservation of the family unit in our complex present-day society. And the family unit is the all-important factor in the preservation of that society itself.'[35]

All the same, Magnusson Grossman's talent appealed broadly to women throughout her career. She designed for professional women like herself, not for the image of the domestic housewife,

unlike many male designers of that period. This may account for why her designs were sought after by single professional women. In light of this, how Magnusson Grossman's work ended up being forgotten remains an interesting question.[36]

Magnusson Grossman was also popular with public figures. Within a year of arriving in LA in 1940, a reporter described an encounter with the kind of professional woman that Magnusson Grossman's work attracted.

> After ten minutes of conversation she noticed a Swedish flag on Mrs. Magnusson Grossman's bracelet, and said:
>
> "Are you Swedish?"
>
> "Yes," said the furniture expert.
>
> "So am I," said the stranger. "My name is Garbo, Greta Garbo."[37]

Other movie star clients included Joan Fontaine and Paulette Goddard, the comedienne Gracie Allen, but also men such as J.P. Seeberg,[38] Frank Sinatra and Paul Trousdale.[39] This proximity to power – and, in particular, the cinematic world – may account for the way she styled herself in media images, as seen in the Frank Bros. advertisement picturing their designers: as the only woman in a collage of eight, her image is that of an actor's headshot (Fig.20). Perhaps this also accounts for why she stated a desire to 'make complete modern film interiors'.[40] This ambition, however, never really materialised, despite the fact that set-designers would often shop at her store as well.

ACTS OF ARCHITECTURE

Through her increasingly sought-after interior design work, Magnusson Grossman's ability to 'modify [M]odernism'[41] to appeal to more mainstream tastes attracted the attention of modernist architects including A. Albert Cooling, Gregory Ain and Paul László, who sought to collaborate with her. Designing domestic residences for public figures, these collaborations provided opportunities for Magnusson Grossman to develop her interior design expertise, to produce bespoke pieces of furniture and to gain a sense

FRANK BROS. *feature prominent contemporary interior design—including the work of such prominent designers as (from top left to right):*

Eames, Saarinen, Robsjohn-Gibbings, Nelson, Martine, Testa, Grossman, Noguchi, Van Keppel, and Green.

2400 AMERICAN AVENUE · LONG BEACH · CALIFORNIA · PHONE LONG BEACH 4-8137

Frank Bros.

20   Frank Bros. advertisement picturing designers, 1949

21   Interior, Trousdale House, Palm Springs, 1947–48. Building designed by architect Allen Siple. Custom furniture designed by Greta Magnusson Grossman and produced by Barker Brothers. Photograph by Maynard L. Parker

of how to work independently as an architect – a skillset she would later rely upon when completing her own private architectural commissions.

For László's home for Texas oilman Charles McGaha, Magnusson Grossman designed a 28-foot coil spring sofa wrapped in four and a half inches of foam, then rubber-covered with down – which she described as 'the most extravagant piece I have ever done'.[42] In contrast, LA housing plots were typically small by today's standards, and Magnusson Grossman became an expert in advising consumers on how to maximise available space: 'One or two extra large sofas will occupy less space, make the room appear larger and actually accommodate more comfortably than will a number of smaller love seats, sofas and chairs.'[43]

Magnusson Grossman's most famous collaboration was with Allen Siple, who designed a house for Paul Trousdale, the Californian real estate developer. Trousdale was behind the creation of Palm Springs, which was lauded in the media as exemplifying the 'New American Look . . . an unmistakable merging of old and new architectural forms to produce new homes that have the first of both period and modern.'[44] The ranch-like interior embodied Magnusson Grossman's philosophy perfectly (Fig.21). 'There is no sense in discarding the old merely because it is not new . . . so many old things mix in very well. So many good things are timeless',[45] she explained in an interview in 1951. This lack of modernist dogma, which tended to privilege the new over the old, was subsequently applied in the house she designed for herself and her husband, Billy, on Waynecrest Drive in Beverly Hills, where she fully transitioned from the role of furniture and interior designer into architect.

HOUSING AS A CATALYST

During the post-war immigration boom, a strategy for housing California's burgeoning population was needed. Sizeable sections of orange grove were removed in order to make way for the tract developments, in what was to be the longest continuous real estate boom in LA's history.[46] Not only did LA need homes for returning war veterans and their new families, but also for the one million emigres who moved to the city after the war, followed by two million more in the 1950s.[47] This demand presented an exciting opportunity for Magnusson Grossman to respond to this need, develop exceptional typological expertise and, given the scale of the demand for housing, gain access to a traditionally male-dominated industry that would previously have proved nearly impossible for a woman to penetrate.

California's recovery from the Depression of the 1930s, coupled with the homes needed by the returning GIs, placed new emphasis upon housing design – and the LA Housing Authority entitled its 1942 fourth report, *Homes for Heroes*. These newly prosperous consumers helped to turn the state of California into a centre for progressive architecture and furnishings throughout the US.[48] As Richard Neutra described it, 'the people of America have found a new mode of living, and southern California, the richest community in the world, is fostering the economical, colorful, casual Californian Way of Life that you may all enjoy'.[49] It should be noted, however, that racist housing covenants restricted the sale of many modern properties and helped to keep the suburbs predominantly white and non-Jewish.[50] The principles of democratic design and consciousness of social values that characterised European modernism were somewhat diminished within the Californian context.

The region also witnessed an abandonment of the wartime 'make do and mend' philosophy with the emergence of disposable synthetics and swiftly obsolete appliances that lacked the biodegradability

of the natural materials that Magnusson Grossman and others liked to incorporate into their interiors and objects. Notwithstanding, Californians still favoured their connection with nature through their surroundings. All of Magnusson Grossman's LA houses embodied her democratic and Scandinavian design philosophy of delivering function, form, sustainability, quality and affordability – uniquely – using a blend of old and new, organic and engineered materials and elements. As much as her work embodied the principles she had absorbed and developed over the past two decades, it also resonated deeply with the modern architecture being developed in California in the wider sphere.

The Case Study House programme – a series of residences sponsored by *Arts & Architecture* magazine that commissioned the likes of Richard Neutra, Raphael Soriano, Craig Ellwood, Charles and Ray Eames, Pierre Koenig, Eero Saarinen, A. Quincy Jones, Edward Killingsworth and Ralph Rapson – likewise shared an over-arching design philosophy. Using the magazine as his tool, editor John Entenza instigated the design of experimental dwellings that challenged the conventions of domestic living. According to architectural critic Reyner Banham: 'The program, the magazine, and a handful of architects really made it appear that Los Angeles was about to contribute to the world not merely odd works of architectural genius but a whole consistent style.'[51] The possible reasons why Entenza never chose to commission Magnusson Grossman to contribute to the programme are discussed later in this chapter, but her architectural designs unquestionably relate to the West Coast ethos.

Almost all of the houses that Magnusson Grossman designed were built upon scenic lots overlooking the canyons and hills that distinguished Los Angeles County. While their facades were always modest, the emphasis was consistently placed upon the extruded interior, designed to de-partition interior from exterior and include nature as part of the domestic realm. Magnusson Grossman took working with nature very seriously, often employing landscape designer Garrett Eckbo, author of *Landscape for Living*,[52] to see the landscape, quite literally, as an extended living space.

In total, Magnusson Grossman would design 28 houses in Los Angeles alone, and another back in Sweden, without ever formally qualifying as an architect. Widely published in an array of significant publications, including *Arts & Architecture* (US), *Architecture d'Aujourd'hui* (France) and *Domus* (Italy), the media's many accounts of several of these houses provide an essential catalogue of their innovative and distinct characteristics. In contrast, mention of her work is largely absent from history books of that period. A detailed analysis of her most significant houses – selected because of the integrity and innovation within their interiors, over other design characteristics – is provided in Chapter 3, where the significance of her work is more deeply interrogated.

NATIONALISM, IDENTITY AND BELONGING

Although Magnusson Grossman's relative obscurity can be largely attributed to the gender politics of her time, other aspects of her identity and life with Billy likely played a part. The Californian context in which Magnusson Grossman operated may have been one of the most creative, expressive and culturally informed across all of the US, but there were wider political forces to contend with – forces which sought to privilege the advancement of a particular section of American society, while disadvantaging others. Magnusson Grossman may have been talented, but her access to marginalised forms of cultural activity was to some extent dependent upon the agency of her husband, whose jazz musicianship positioned him within a community of largely African-American artists who were facing inequalities of their own.

In the 1940s, America was deeply racially divided. Even in California, it took until 1979 to fully desegregate schools. Yet, when the Magnusson Grossmans arrived in 1941, the horror of war had matured LA, transitioning it from the 'gangly, awkward star-struck youngster of the 1920s and the troubled, searching adolescent of the 1930s, into a city that exuded confidence in its emerging industrial power'.[53] For Magnusson Grossman, confronting discrimination on the grounds of nationality, religion and gender became possible from within the community of creatives she and her husband had joined – creatives who were sensitised to injustice and committed to resisting it. Moreover, as a white, blonde-haired and attractive woman, Magnusson Grossman would

have had to contend with the challenge of being an acceptable 'face' of design by women, while simultaneously struggling to be taken seriously by the same audience. For example, in one account, Magnusson Grossman is described as 'a very vital, attractive blond type around 40, feminine in manner yet strong and vigorous in her approach to her work. It is reflective of her early training in man's domain.'[54]

In 1952, the US State Department wrote to Magnusson Grossman to inform her that a profile about her originally written for the *American Artist* magazine would be distributed to the international media in 75 different countries via the department's Overseas Program, in order to 'give people of other countries a true picture of the United States and the American way of life'.[55] It seems ironic that Magnusson Grossman could be marketed abroad as an all-American icon, but the US media resolutely ensured she carried the Swedish prefix in articles intended for a domestic audience. Examples include: Rose Henderson, 'A Swedish Furniture Designer in America: An Interview with Greta Magnusson Grossman', *American Artist*, December 1951,[56] and 'Good Design Is Appearance Plus Comfort: Swedish-born Designer Works Toward the Perfect Combination', *Western Upholstery Furniture & Bedding*, April 1953.[57]

INDUSTRIAL DESIGN INNOVATION

Like many great architects, designing architecture and interiors alone was never enough for Magnusson Grossman. Design products – from furniture, lighting and fabrics to the portable aluminium oven she designed for Alcoa's (Aluminum Corporation of America) Forecast programme – reveal an inventive relentlessness and rigour that no one discipline could satiate. During the 1950s, Magnusson Grossman designed furnishings for a variety of companies and her many products were sold in stores alongside the work of enduringly famous architects and designers such as Charles and Ray Eames and Eero Saarinen. Inversely, some of Magnusson Grossman's more popular pieces – in proportion to the press attention they received – were produced in relatively small numbers. Some of her most enduring and iconic work was for the Ralph O. Smith lighting company, which employed only two machinists during its ten-year existence,[58] and for whom she designed the the Cobra lamp (Plates 5, 17 and 18) and Grasshopper floor lamp (Plate 19), both of which won MoMA's Design Designation Award in 1950 (Cobra).[59] Another of her most important clients was Glenn of California, a company comprised of less than ten employees which typically produced around 200 pieces per design. In 1952, Magnusson Grossman launched the 62-series for the company, a range of living, dining and bedroom furniture so-called because it was considered a potent symbol of the future, ten years ahead of its time.[60]

When Magnusson Grossman arrived in the US in 1940, a boom in petroleum-based materials and product manufacturing offered a new opportunity for experimentation. Seeing their unrealised potential, Magnusson Grossman sought to experiment with laminate surfaces for the home and explored innovative ways of blending them with traditional Swedish materials and forms. Subsequently, this approach directly informed the design of a drop-leaf coffee table in walnut and plastic laminate (1952) (Plate 6) and a set of dressers in walnut (1952) (Plate 20).

These pieces of furniture illustrate the tensions and contradictions between the present and the past, the vernacular and the modern, engendering a sense of lightness stood out against the solid, heavy and sturdy furniture that was typical of the time in more conventional stores.[61] Similarly, her 1952 walnut-framed room screen (Plate 21) – featuring primary-coloured balls impaled upon a wire grid – alluded to the astronautical aspirations of the era and intriguingly resembles the Hang It All hooks of husband and wife designers Charles and Ray Eames, launched a year later in 1953 (whether there was a conscious appropriation is not altogether clear).

Magnusson Grossman's bestsellers ultimately proved to be the Ralph O. Smith double-shaded Cobra lamp (1948–49) (Fig.22) and the Grasshopper floor lamp (1947–48) (Figs 23 and 24), the latter of which is considered her best-known piece today. The Cobra lamp aesthetic is not dissimilar to the Red Kaiser Idell 6786 Bauhaus desk lamp by Christian Dell, also designed during the 1950s, although the question of who influenced who is equally hard to resolve.

22   Double-shaded Cobra table lamp, produced by Ralph O. Smith, 1948–49

23   Double-shaded Grasshopper floor lamp, produced by Ralph O. Smith, 1947–48. Photograph by Julius Shulman

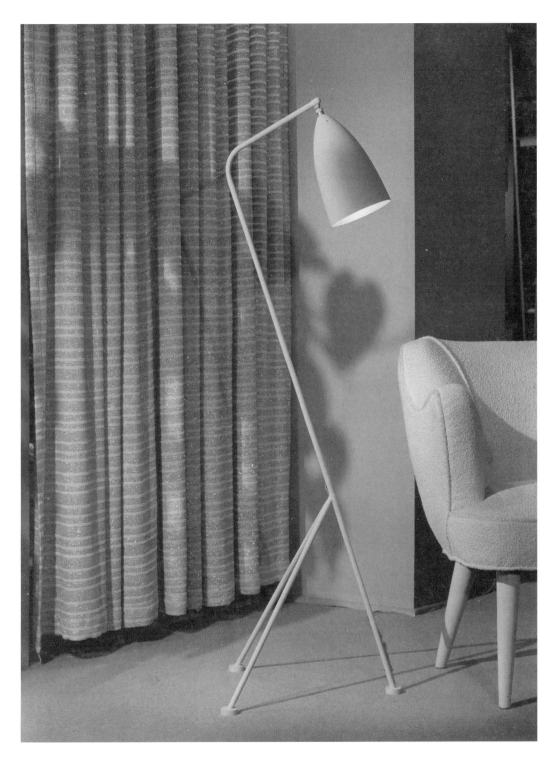

24   Grasshopper floor lamp, produced by Ralph O. Smith, 1947–48. Photograph by Julius Shulman

RETROSPECTION AND RE-LAUNCH

As a testimony to the enduring legacy of Magnusson Grossman's work, eight of her lamps, seven of her soft seats and her 62 Desk have been relaunched by Swedish furniture manufacturers, Gubi. The company's CEO and owner, Jacob Gubi, took the decision to re-launch some of Magnusson Grossman's products after an encounter with R & Company's exhibition of her work in their New York City gallery, curated by Evan Snyderman. As Gubi explained, 'Magnusson Grossman's work was too important, and too desirable by today's standards, to be available to collectors alone. By relaunching her work with some minor manufacturing modifications, it becomes more affordable for more people, which is Gubi's democratic approach.'[62]

In contrast to her industrial design, Magnusson Grossman's architectural legacy is especially under-recognised, a subject we discuss in more detail in Chapter 4. With most of her architecture projects either demolished and redeveloped or substantially altered, despite incremental posthumous recognition for her spatial contribution, the (professional) conservation movement, as well as the (academic) canon, sadly lack Jacob Gubi's 'recognition by remanufacture' approach to the work of such an important designer.

RESIGNING AND RESIGNATION

By 1960, Magnusson Grossman was more successful than ever before. She was not only sought after by companies in Sweden and the US, but by a media that looked to California to determine the next trend in furniture design and by cultural institutions keen to feature her work in their exhibitions. These included the Pasadena Art Museum's *California Design* series, the *Pacifica Designs* exhibition in northern California, the Walker Art Center in Minneapolis, the Museum of Science and Industry in Chicago, the de Young Museum in San Francisco and the *H55* exhibition at Helsingborg, the latter of which attracted more than a million people, despite the fact that Magnusson Grossman did not even attend.[63]

In addition to this, Magnusson Grossman began teaching furniture design at ArtCenter College of Design in Pasadena[64] and at the University of California (UCLA), Los Angeles campus, in 1957. She resigned from her UCLA position in 1963 after only six years – perhaps due to disciplinary frustration or a dislike of teaching. When invited to reflect upon her young students in an *LA Times* magazine article in 1960, Magnusson Grossman questioned why they seemed to 'look for security' when 'the easiest way to show what you can do is to do it on your own'[65] – echoing the independence but also the isolation Magnusson Grossman faced throughout her career. Withdrawing from teaching is one of several indications that she was becoming disillusioned with the California design scene. In the same article, Magnusson Grossman went on to state that:

> We have fallen into a period of decadence . . . back 100 to 200 years for design themes. We have lost our searching for design [*sic*] that fits the time we are living in. And our design doesn't start from within, it starts from without. A designer thinks that if he puts a face on his piece of furniture that is modern. But a house that has plumbing is modern. Current design is not thought through and it is not original.[66]

OBSCURITY AND EXCLUSION

Within a few months of the 1960 *LA Times* interview, Magnusson Grossman and her husband Billy left LA (Fig.25) in favour of the more relaxed and detached San Diego, cutting her ties to the design industry and her community of friends and collaborators. Thereafter, Magnusson Grossman abruptly stopped designing and focused instead on painting and playing bridge. Very little is known about the second half of her life. Billy suffered from ill health and died in 1979, leaving her a widow for a further 20 years before she too passed away.[67] When interviewed about Magnusson Grossman's successful career, her San Diego friends reported that she had never once mentioned it – which we posit could be because the memory of it was painful in some way. Whatever her reasons, the cost of building and maintaining her position within the industry would have been formidable.

25   Photograph of the Magnusson Grossmans at
Claircrest Drive, Beverly Hills, c.1960

While in California, Magnusson Grossman often
built on spec, living with Billy in the properties
until they found a buyer – reflecting the scale of
demand for housing and the strength of the market
for more middle-class, innovatively designed,
detached properties. Indeed, Magnusson
Grossman's houses were published across the
architectural press and commended as much as
the Case Study projects. That she was excluded
from this programme – despite her work being
not just equal, but at times arguably superior, to
those included – may well account for why she
stopped practising in the late 1950s, turning to
painting instead. Certainly, when scrutinising the
chronology of many of the Case Study houses, it
is evident that her ideas were being developed
within them, and to great acclaim. The justification
for this exclusion – and for her peers choosing to
refer to her as a designer rather than an architect
– is presumed to be on the basis that she lacked
formal, American, architectural qualifications,
sanctioned by the American Institute of Architects
(AIA).[68]

Magnusson Grossman was one of only a handful
of women in the design business and she was more
exceptional still to be running an architecture
and design firm as a sole female practitioner.
In addition to this, her husband Billy had failed
to match the success of his musical career in
Stockholm and as a consequence, Magnusson
Grossman's ability to operate as what is generally –
and offensively – labelled 'breadwinner' became an
imperative. Billy decided to contribute to his wife's
career and in some reports is characterised as her
business manager. This sits in contrast to the wives
of architects whose roles are often described as
that of a secretary – enablers but never managers
– if their creative or practical contribution is ever
acknowledged at all. Indeed, few women designers
were independently successful during this period,
relying instead upon creative partnerships for their
careers to flourish, as the careers and reputation
of Ray Eames (married to Charles) and Olga Lee
(married to Milo Baughman) illustrate. Of the
handful of women designers active during this
time, Magnusson Grossman was the only one
designing houses.

3   Living in a Modern Way

'In the industrialized West, the design of the interior has been conceptualized as a domestic and amateur phenomenon, and the domestic interior has been conceptualized as a feminine realm.'

Grace Lees-Maffei (2008)[1]

'The emergence of the interior framed domesticity in its modern form.'

Charles Rice (2006)[2]

26   A typical southern California bungalow

The Second World War had a disruptive effect upon the design of the domestic interior in Europe and the United States. The impact of the 'war effort' upon manufacturing, as well as the absence of men who were otherwise assigned military duties, served to allow women greater agency in organisation and decoration. Early modernism's yearnings towards open-plan, light-flooded continuous spaces with few partitions meant that rooms previously classified as women's spaces – for example, the kitchen or scullery – had dissolved.

Before modernism, California's affection for single-storey dwelling had spawned an entire typology, known as the 'California Bungalow', that became popular throughout the United States from 1910 to 1939. Typically detached, thoroughly internally partitioned and often afforded an Art Deco or more generic Arts and Crafts flourish, these dwellings were marketed and sold by companies such as Sears which had 'established themselves as purveyors of the ready-cut home' (Fig.26).[3]

When modernist housing's flowing interiors began appearing in Californian homes, they sat in stark contrast to the reassuringly gender-segregated bungalow, ushering in an era where domestic dominance had to be asserted rather than assumed, and the default was to assume that each 'area' – as opposed to room – was democratised rather than

delineated. Perhaps this is why many returning Second World War veterans were left to assume that 'the only residential program a man could imagine ruling [was] the house of the bachelor'.[4]

In 1953, while Magnusson Grossman was busy completing the Hart House in the Hollywood Knolls (whose structure remains intact at the time of writing) (Plate 16), Hugh Hefner founded *Playboy* magazine, a publication whose success can be largely attributed to the extent to which it addresses anxieties over diminishing masculine dominance. Perhaps this is what prompted writer George Wagner to assert that the post-Second World War domestic interior became 'the most intense and gendered site of commodity consumption in the mechanical and electronic era of privatisation'.[5] According to Wagner, *Playboy* projected a 'fantasy escape' from a world where family life took precedence in the home, and the 'office' was synonymous with earning money. 'The image of the bachelor's life advanced by *Playboy* provided a private fantasy escape for the man whose home had been appropriated as the domain of wife and family and whose office was the site of a definitive reality – the wage.'[6]

There were, by that time, two million more wives in the American labour force than there had been at the peak of wartime production,[7] which perhaps explains – but does not justify – why, in 1953, *Playboy* saw fit to bemoan that, although until 'a couple of generations ago, this was a man's world [now] nothing could be further from the truth'.[8] The story also branded working women as 'gold diggers', even though the contradiction between being both a gold digger and a wage earner could not have been more apparent. It seems that *Playboy* writers felt particularly threatened by women's increased presence within the workplace, the arts and, especially, the home. In a 1958 article, *Playboy* columnist and author Phillip Wylie characterised the modern American home as a 'boudoir-kitchen nursery, dreamed up for women and by women and as if males did not exist as males'.[9] Evidently, modernism – even with all its sexist canons – proved emasculating. Understanding the nature of the gender-political backdrop against which Magnusson Grossman worked serves to further advance arguments that her talent was exceptional, given she was able to thrive despite these odds.

If we consider the histories of modernism, and the role of the interior within this discourse, it is clear that where architecture is celebrated as the ultimate expression of a functionalist and egalitarian philosophy, the interior is rather overlooked. Although the domestic interior was the site of scientific experimentation during the 20th century – Grete Schütte-Lihotzky's Frankfurt Kitchen from 1926 (Fig.27), for example – the interior itself had little agency within this. Instead,

27 Frankfurt Kitchen by Grete Schütte-Lihotzky, 1926–27

it was reduced to the accommodation of everyday banality – a sequence of spaces that were often framed around a minimum set of requirements facilitating the existence of the 'modern nomad'. With reference to art historian Christopher Reed, who has argued that 'heroic avant-gardes, and Le Corbusier in particular, defined modernism as the antithesis of the domestic',[10] Charles Rice prefers to focus on modernism's role in understanding the interior in terms of image and not function – 'an interior is formed in a particular perceptual mode, rather than being identifiable in terms of enclosure and encasing'.[11]

In an April 2019 article for *Dezeen* entitled, 'The Vision of the Home as a Tranquil Respite from Labour Is a Patriarchal Fantasy',[12] curator and writer Phineas Harper questions whether the nuclear family home is 'an architectural tool of repression and social control', and a 'deterministic form of architecture which stifles individual and collective potential [that] . . . enforce[s] a particular social structure, and . . . hardwires divisions in labour, gender and class into the built fabric of our cities'.[13] Certainly during the mid-20th century, when designing for the home flourished as a commercial venture, we can see the origins of this determinism where the kitchen was reinforced as the site of women's work. Citing Pier Vittorio Aureli and Maria Shéhérazade Giudici's essay, 'Familiar Horror: Toward a Critique of Domestic Space', Harper points to Aureli and Guidici's statement that 'Family roles we consider today to be strictly natural: the titles of father, mother, son, or heir had nothing to do with biology and everything to do with the rationale of preserving the ownership, and thus the order, of the house.'[14]

Designing the home in order to maintain this hierarchy persists today, despite technologies that seek to liberate women from this closed structure by networking the home through an Internet of Things, as well as narratives that test the home as a hybrid 'third place'[15] – or, complexified by the knowledge economy, even a 'fourth place' – somewhere that 'blurs the frontier, within the same space, of the first (home), second (work), and third place making the space, a place in itself'.[16] Such spaces, suggests economic geographer Arnault Morrison, facilitate social interaction and collaborative practices that enable 'the exchange of tacit knowledge'.[17] Architect and curator Terence Riley's notion of the 'un-private house' is also pertinent here as it suggests an environment that is entirely porous – open to the flow of data that passes through it.[18] Where Magnusson Grossman sits in relation to this discussion about both the place of the interior within the context of historical modernism – and indeed its role within a feminist spatial discourse – is that, instead of shifting the narrative of the interior towards the public sphere, she is able to reframe work as a domestic activity. It is our contention that this is part of Magnusson Grossman's legacy.

Greta Magnusson Grossman's career as a designer of furniture and, later, houses specifically addresses the domestic interior as the natural habitat of the 'modern' woman. The homes she designed for herself and her husband to live in can perhaps be considered her most experimental – indeed her 'most special'.[19] In her essay, 'Modern Living', in *A Car and Some Shorts*, curator Karin Åberg Waern offers an in-depth analysis of Magnusson Grossman's designs for these important spaces: the apartment on Storskärsgatan (Stockholm) and the houses at Waynecrest Drive and Claircrest Drive (Los Angeles). The essay highlights what she sees as the uniqueness of these homes, and in particular, the ways in which they connect the living spaces together.[20] Certainly there is an intimacy to these environments that is autobiographical, as with many homes designed by the occupier, exposing the essence of who we are. In these houses, Magnusson Grossman was able to explore ideas about domestic living and test them *in situ*: these spaces were conceived as environments to both live and work long before the design industry 'invented' live/work spaces in the late 20th century.

In the 19th century, the bourgeoisie had established the idea of home as domestic, private and feminine and the city beyond as the public, masculine realm (even though there were clearly spaces within the domestic sphere, such as studies, which operated as protected masculine enclaves, and feminine spaces within the city, such as arcades and department stores, that offered a safe space for 'respectable' women to be in public). Magnusson Grossman, as did many of her contemporaries, designed interiors that broke down these public and private binaries

in two ways: first, through the amalgamation of work and home; second – and this is something that is almost exclusive to Magnusson Grossman – by opening up the home to the public gaze. The sheer proliferation of interviews and magazine articles that underpin her early career in Stockholm often picture the Magnusson Grossmans 'at home', commenting on the ways in which Greta's designs facilitate a particular kind of domesticity that is framed around the glamour of the dinner party. Such events enabled Magnusson Grossman to encourage potential clients into commissioning her to recreate this domestic bliss – as a networking strategy it appears to have been remarkably successful.

Later articles from the US also revel in picturing Magnusson Grossman in her own home. Where advertising images of women in the home during the 1940s and 1950s conflate gender and domesticity, Magnusson Grossman appears uniquely able to inhabit her domestic environment from a position of power – as both comfortable in but separate from this space. For Magnusson Grossman is mistress *of* and *in* her home and within this space her gender is secondary to her role as designer. If we look carefully at the photograph taken by architectural photographer Julius Shulman for Alcoa in 1959, with Magnusson Grossman at her desk looking slightly to her right of the camera lens, we sense a designer in control of her world, not a woman constrained by it (Fig.28).

For Magnusson Grossman, her workspace is the focal point of her home – something that did not go unnoticed at the time. Elsa Pehrson, in her 1944 article 'West Coast Designer' for *American Swedish Monthly*, writes: 'in the center of the living-room Greta Magnusson Grossman has placed her drawing table. Drawings and blueprints are scattered all over it.'[21] Pehrson is even more intrigued by Magnusson Grossman's approach to design: 'This Swedish decorator believes that to design furniture you must be a psychologist . . . She wants her customers to be the co-creators of their own homes, not merely the passive buyers of someone else's ideas, however good they may be.'[22] Where many of her largely male contemporaries looked to enhance their status through the accumulation of authored projects, Magnusson Grossman recognised the need for design as a collaborative exercise.

28   Greta Magnusson Grossman. Photograph by Julius Schulman for the
Aluminum Corporation of America, 1959

ORIGINS OF A PROFESSION

Magnusson Grossman's design practice, both in Stockholm and later in Los Angeles, was forged at a time when the profession of interior designer had begun to attain a new level of respectability. Rice traces the origins of the design of domestic space back to the early 1800s, citing Charles Percier and Pierre Fontaine's *Recueil de Décorations Intérieurs* [Collection of Interior Decoration] of 1801 and Hope's *Household Furniture and Interior Decoration* of 1807 as inaugural works to present the field.[23] These texts identified the domestic interior as an indeterminate space where both architects and upholsterers staked a claim for territorial rights.

Design historian Penny Sparke also deliberates on the origins of the planning of the interior as a site of professional practice, and in particular its post-war expansion as a specialised field. Sparke's thesis suggests that the origins of this practice were to be found in modernism, which created an ideological split between interior design and the then maligned activities of the interior decorator that were linked to feminine pursuits within the home.[24] In the post-war era it was common for interior designers to have been educated as architects – the principle of designing everything 'from the spoon to the city'[25] (a phrase adopted by Italian architect Ernesto Rogers in the 1950s, although originally coined by Herman Muthesius while Chairman of the Deutscher Werkbund between 1910 and 1916), which meant that the interior was to be absorbed into the overall task of designing buildings. Although this delineation of the interior as a site of valid professional practice offers legitimacy to what had previously been conceived as a hobby, Sparke points to the crux of what has proved, in the long-term, to be a significant problem for interiors as both a commercial practice and an intellectual discourse – legitimising interior design through its connection to architecture rather than to the craft and industrial design practices that birthed it. By subsuming the interior into architectural practice, it lost its autonomy.

Of course, design historians are themselves also culpable in this perception of the interior as an adjunct to architecture, 'privileging'[26] the work of key modernists and handing down histories of

20th-century design which have tended to exclude the work of women in particular. Penny Sparke herself, writing in 2008, rather overlooks the contribution of Ray Eames, wife of Charles Eames, to the modernist canon. The chapter on 'The Designed Interior' in her text *The Modern Interior*, although eloquent in its analysis of the role of design in the shaping of domestic space in the mid-20th century, tends towards celebrating the work of Charles in this narrative. Here is Sparke describing the Eames' own home (Fig.29):

> He filled the interior with his own furniture designs and numerous mementos which have been linked to Eames's commitment to the notion of 'functioning decoration', an important characteristic of the new, humanized face of Modernism. The high levels of decoration in the interior of Eames's Santa Monica house have been attributed to the intervention of Charles' wife Ray. A continuum undoubtedly existed in the couple's minds between their domestic spaces and their work environments.[27]

Although Ray Eames' contribution to the canon of modernism is acknowledged elsewhere – for example in Pat Kirkham's 1998 essay, 'Humanizing Modernism: The Crafts, "Functioning Decoration" and the Eameses', where she suggests that Ray Eames was actually the more progressive partner in the practice – the role of women in histories of 20th-century design remains under-explored.[28] The underlying argument of Sparke's writing on interior design as professional practice remains clear, nonetheless: that the period between 1945 and 1960 witnessed a reinvention of the interior as a hybrid of the private and the public spheres; and that this reinvention was disseminated through mass media, which looked to frame this 'progressive modernity'.[29] And for Sparke too, this discourse is profoundly gendered. Although the professionalisation of interior design during this period was reflected in a close affinity with architecture, this also ensured the marginalisation of the interior decorator:

> In spite of the fact that they continued to work with wealthy, upper-class clients for the most part, and mostly, but not exclusively, in the

29   Case Study House No. 8 – the Eames House, 1949

domestic arena, professional interior decorators were significantly marginalized. Latter-day modernists saw the work of the decorators as feminized, trivial and superficial and believed that it over-emphasized the role of textiles and ignored that of architectural structure.[30]

For Sparke and other historians of the interior, including ourselves, the idea of 'interior decoration' 'has still to be recuperated'.[31]

MASS MEDIA

The role that the media played in making the designed interior accessible to a mass audience was especially important in rebalancing the hierarchy of the private and public spheres that had come about during industrialisation in the 19th century. In 1941, the Museum of Modern Art in New York staged an exhibition called *Organic Design in Home Furnishings*, featuring room-sets that combined domestic objects with those of the workplace and introducing the designs of the Eames' and other significant practitioners in the field to the public gaze. The exhibition was the outcome of a competition curated by Eliot Noyes, which called for 'organic design' as a 'harmonious organization of the parts within the whole, according to structure, material, and purpose. Within this definition there can be no vain ornamentation or superfluity, but the part of beauty is none-the-less great – in ideal choice of material, in visual refinement, and in the rational elegance of things intended for use.'[32]

MoMA's Good Design awards, which took place annually between 1950 and 1955, were also significant in establishing modern craft and design within sight of a public audience. Edgar Kaufman, Jr., who was Director of MoMA's Industrial Design department during this period, headed up the initiative which, in conjunction with Merchandise Mart, staged five exhibitions to display the competition entries for the awards. They also developed an endorsement tag for the designs on display, which operated as a tool for promoting modern home furnishings within the marketplace. Magnusson Grossman won an award for her Cobra lamp in 1950 and for a chair made by Glenn of California in 1952, which were thereafter retailed with the Good Design seal and came to rank among her most successful products.

The exposure of modern design in exhibitions and in the press at the time achieved something which early modernists had failed to address – the dissemination of innovative design thinking to a public audience. Mary Davis Gillies, in her 1948 handbook, *All About Modern Decorating*, offered practical advice on how to assemble the modern home on a reasonable budget. For Davis Gillies, social status could be improved through the implementation of some straightforward strategies that included the streamlining of one's possessions and the eradication of a separate dining room.[33] Other depictions of the modern interior at the time are more playful. George Nelson, in *Interiors* magazine, described it as 'comprising "a large rubber plant . . . a couple of Aalto stools and armchairs, a modern coffee table, and a few pieces of prehistoric-looking pottery"'.[34]

Swedish design during this period also attracted significant coverage, both in Europe and North America. The 1939 Swedish Pavilion at the New York World's Fair introduced the achievements of Swedish designers to a largely American audience whose fascination for all things Swedish was propagated by the press and within the pages of a number of contemporary publications. Sparke makes reference to the furniture of Bruno Mathsson in the apartment of Philip Goodwin in New York and illustrated in the 1946 book, *Inside Your Home*, as particularly influential. Here the interiors depicted are simple yet comfortable spaces in which to live – where the furniture is at one with the environment and its inhabitants.

THE ARCHIVE

As we have written in the introduction to this book, the documentation of Magnusson Grossman's body of work as a professional designer largely exists inside the archive held by R & Company, a gallery founded in 1997 in New York City with a mission to increase awareness and interest in collectable design through research, exhibitions and publications. Our reading and interpretation of Magnusson Grossman's work was based on these archival materials and, thus, relies on the articles and images that depict it, rather than through the work itself. We will consider the legacies of Magnusson Grossman's work, both as reproduced furniture and in terms of the remnants of buildings still visible in the LA landscape, but first, it is worth examining how photographs themselves offer up her designs for consumption. In many ways, Greta Magnusson Grossman's work *is* the images and not simply the actual spaces and objects that she produced.

According to Rice, it was Adolf Loos who first recognised 'the doubleness of the interior, that it is at once image and spatial condition'.[35] Architectural historian and theorist Beatriz Colomina has also written extensively on this subject, both in her essay on Loos and Le Corbusier, 'The Split Wall: Domestic Voyeurism', and in her book *Privacy and Publicity: Modern Architecture as Mass Media*, which suggests that architecture is shaped through the media that frames it. Indeed, the receptiveness of Magnusson Grossman's work to the static photographic image is not dissimilar to the 'Instagrammable' environments that are constructed today. Hers are stage-sets designed to communicate status and fashionability, largely devoid of human inhabitation. Sometimes the designer is pictured seated at her desk, but for the most part, images of her work also foreground her functionalist designs as images rather than spaces.

The ongoing concern for the depiction of the interior which, for the most part, is only rendered up for public scrutiny when it is described in the pages of a glossy magazine, reduces it instantly to a discussion of style rather than content and meaning. As such, the interior is made available to 'commercial exploitation'.[36] The writings of philosopher and essayist, Walter Benjamin, in particular his thesis on photography, are also explored in Rice's thesis on the interior and offer indications to understand the present discussion. Rice suggests that photography captures the 'event' of the interior but in doing so removes the 'aura' of its contents.[37] For Le Corbusier, continues Rice, the photograph goes further: by extinguishing all evidence of inhabitation, it arrives at a version of domesticity that is 'post-interior'.[38] For Colomina, this is where 'modern architecture as mass media emerges'.[39]

The photographs of Magnusson Grossman's interiors, however, sustain our belief in their success as homes. Despite the absence of actual figures within the frame, these images nevertheless capture a domestic scene that is both authentic and marketable. Not surprisingly, nine of Magnusson Grossman's houses were published in *Arts & Architecture*, and it seems clear that editor John Entenza was interested in her work and keen to promote it within the pages of his magazine. Certainly, the journal was significant in establishing the careers of a number of architects and designers practising in and around Los Angeles at the time, but it also curated a distinctly Californian aesthetic that has been written about extensively since.

Yet, despite actively promoting Magnusson Grossman's work, Entenza – as we have established in Chapter 2 – apparently never approached her to take part in the famous Case Study programme. Interestingly, other than the Eames House, no women appear to have been

involved in this significant project. In any event, one writer has suggested that the Case Study Houses programme 'did not encourage heroics; what it asked for was service'.[40] Rather than pushing the boundaries of contemporary house design, the programme seems to have produced aesthetic exercises in form and materiality. Although influential within the field, as single-family units, these homes did not offer any meaningful solution to the wider problem of housing the masses and perhaps did not intrigue Magnusson Grossman as something different from what she was already doing through her professional practice.

The Case Study Houses programme was also not unique – during the 1940s, the Walker Art Center in Minneapolis instigated the *Idea House* exhibitions to investigate and test new thinking in domestic design. Like the Case Study Houses (yet pre-dating them), the Idea House also adopted the single-family dwelling unit as its typology of choice, but looked to 'disrupt its conventional role, encouraging visitors to borrow from a range of solutions, rather than accepting a prepackaged, standardized home design'.[41] The exhibitions also recognised the commercial potential of domestic design and, in many ways, can be seen as advertisements for what Colomina describes as 'the commercialization of domestic life'.[42] Even if Magnusson Grossman was not aware of programmes such as this, it must be emphasised how her trajectory and professional persona were informed by all these experiences.

A FEMINIST AGENDA?

In her essay for the 2000 exhibition of Magnusson Grossman's work held at R & Company in New York, Lily Kane discusses the challenges Magnusson Grossman must have faced throughout her career in terms of her gender. Kane references the Swedish newspaper and magazine articles that document this period and highlight how surprising it was to find a woman working outside of the field of textiles, let alone running her own practice.[43] Magnusson Grossman's career as a designer, and later architect, was forged within this context, yet she seems to have been aware of her position, stating in one interview that 'it was often a drawback to be a woman, but it kept you on your toes. You had to be one step ahead or else.'[44] It appears that Magnusson Grossman was able to construct her professional life as separate from, rather than part of, her private life and, although her domestic environment provided the backdrop to her work, she seems to have remained independent from it.

In her depiction of the history of interior design as a profession, designer and historian Lucinda Kaukas Havenhand discusses the relationship between female identity and domestic life. Referencing the writings of architect Karen Franck and her ideas regarding 'women's ways of knowing',[45] Kaukas Havenhand suggests that women tend to think collaboratively, de-stabilising the traditional binary divisions between public and private; work and home; male and female. A feminist design process therefore facilitates the removal of hierarchy within the designer/client/ user relationship, enables physical and visual porosity across space, and merges together subjective and objective information.[46] Within this context we can begin to frame Magnusson Grossman's own practice as an emerging feminist.

Magnusson Grossman's identity as a designer remains, however, tempered by her gender rather than freed from it; and, although successful as a female architect/designer, she was operating in a world in which few practitioners had the opportunity to explore design as an intellectual activity. Although participating in exhibitions that opened up design discourse to those actually doing it, rather than simply thinking about it, Magnusson Grossman's relative success was commercial. In her early professional life in Sweden she was invited to participate in exhibitions and events that explored modern design ideas, but her career in LA did not fulfil its potential in terms of influencing others through teaching and other academic exercises. For those designers specialising in the field of domestic interiors, or even interiors *per se*, working life was – and to some extent still is – geared towards industry rather than the academy.

The hierarchy within the field of the built environment has always privileged architecture over interior design, and this narrative is entirely gendered. As we have written elsewhere, the interior continues to be 'marginalised within critical discourse' and remains professionally adrift.[47] The validity of interior design has always been questioned by those bodies and institutions that place it in opposition to architecture.

Magnusson Grossman, working across both disciplines, would have found herself navigating through this complex scenario. Although her later career saw her commissioned to design sixteen houses, the fact that these either no longer exist, have been substantially adapted, or have, in the past, been attributed to Magnusson Grossman's contemporaries evidences both the invisibility of women's authorship as well as the relative marginality of domestic architecture in comparison to other typologies. Many of her largely male contemporaries, who gained recognition in their careers for architecture typologies more visible in the public realm, were invited to contribute to the Case Study Houses programme – now viewed as a badge of honour. At the same time, despite Magnusson Grossman's evident expertise in the field of domestic architecture, these successes appeared to carry little weight when it came to addressing the important business of rethinking the home as an idea. Her architectural portfolio remains marginal and marginalised.

HOME AND OFFICE

The home as a place of work was the norm in Western societies for centuries, but that began to change during the 19th century, when work increasingly took place in the new factories of the Industrial Revolution, and the home started being viewed as fundamentally domestic and unmonetised.[48] While finance and commerce, as middle-class activities, had been sited away from the home for much longer, domestic space had traditionally remained the site of 'women's work'.

The early 20th century witnessed an even greater shift when new, modern thinking ushered in an era of conceiving the home as a 'machine for living in', a phrase coined by Le Corbusier in his 1923 manifesto text *Vers une architecture* [Towards a New Architecture]. And while the

Swiss-born architect mainly tested his theories in singular homes, it is in some of the social housing projects developed in the 1920s and 1930s that we find the best case studies for analysis of the real conditions under which modernist ideas could be tested. In Germany, the modernist project sprang into life with the building of *Neues Frankfurt* [New Frankfurt] – an extensive programme of affordable public housing built between 1925 and 1930 under the stewardship of architect Ernst May. The kitchens that architect Grete Schütte-Lihotsky designed for the scheme aimed to reduce domestic labour and revolutionised their role within the home. In 1929, CIAM, the Congrès Internationaux d'Architecture Moderne [International Congress of Modern Architecture], staged a conference named 'Die Wohnung für das Existenzminimum' [The Dwelling for Minimal Existence], focusing global attention on the Frankfurt experiment, and setting space standards for dwelling needs moving forward.

Despite its ambitions, the modern movement retained some traditional characteristics that had defined domesticity until that point. Le Corbusier's desire to bring the efficiency of the machine to everyday life suppressed what were considered outdated modes of inhabitation and behaviour, but the home nevertheless remained a distinct environment designed to structure and frame domestic activity. Meanwhile, as a study into the future of the home, the housing built in Frankfurt was largely concerned with the act of dwelling rather than testing the relationship between living and working that we begin to see from 1930 onwards.

Magnusson Grossman's early career in Sweden during the 1930s presented a number of opportunities to test her own ideas about the home. As described in Chapter 1, these exercises in exploring 'living in a modern way'[49] looked to challenge accepted norms regarding the organisation of domestic space, as well as address the structure of the family unit. For Magnusson Grossman, it seemed only sensible that domestic arrangements should enable the overlap of the private and public realms: why shouldn't home function as the site of work?

Magnusson Grossman was nevertheless a product of her time and still held on to a traditional

view of family as the focus of society. In an interview given to the *Los Angeles Times* in 1954, she states:

> I feel it is the all-important thing in the preservation of the family unit in our complex present-day society. And the family unit still is the all-important factor in the preservation of that society itself . . . The wife and mother in the servantless home of today must face a minimum of housework if she is going to be the vital central force in her family unit.[50]

Although clearly holding progressive views with regards to her own place as a woman in her profession, her attitude towards female domestic work remained framed by societal expectations.

FUNCTIONING DECORATION

Another fundamental aspect of Magnusson Grossman's approach to assembling the domestic landscape involved what the Eames' identified as 'functioning decoration'. Design historian Pat Kirkham suggests that the couple's fascination with 'stuff' had its origins in the Arts and Crafts Movement and its ethos of finding beauty in everyday things.[51] The phrase 'functioning decoration' certainly gave validity to the practice of ornamenting the home with objects that embellish the interior rather than simply operating as useful to everyday existence. Furthermore, the purpose of 'functioning decoration' was identified by the Eameses as offering an 'extra-cultural surprise'.[52] This act of humanising the interior through the introduction of found things was inspired by Ray Eames' interest in what is now known as 'femmage' – a feminist form of collage that utilises crafts such as sewing and appliqué that are traditionally seen as women's work. Kirkham describes this approach to assembling objects within the interior as 'object-orientated', offering a curated collection of objects independent of their origin – which, suggests Kirkham, is not as benign as it sounds, but rather a clear act of 'cultural imperialism'.[53]

For Magnusson Grossman, the process of constructing the interior also began with objects. Her training as an industrial designer and maker meant that in framing domestic life, her interiors and indeed her architecture were very much tuned in to the placement of personal possessions within the space – similar to the Eames' strategy of functioning decoration, although not articulated in the same way. For Magnusson Grossman, such objects might be inherited or acquired over time, their usefulness embedded in their emotional content as much as in their functional purpose. In an interview given to *American Artist* in 1951, Magnusson Grossman exclaims: 'If a thing is useful, use it! . . . Do not throw it away just because it is old!'[54] In examining period photographs, it becomes clear that the objects that are contained within the Magnusson Grossmans' home environment are essential to the construction of the domestic mise-en-scène.

AT HOME IN SWEDEN

The apartment in which the Magnusson Grossmans lived, in Gärdet, Stockholm (Plate 1), was located in a housing development designed by Albin Stark, c.1931. The development consisted of *lamellar* slabs and low-rise tower blocks next to a generously sized park – as discussed in Chapter 1. Karin Åberg Waern describes it as 'a fine example of Swedish functionalism',[55] where apartment interiors were organised according to function, with a clear separation between the kitchen and the living space. It seems that although the Magnusson Grossmans were clearly attracted to the development in terms of its location and *funkis* aesthetic (Swedish for functionalism, as discussed in Chapter 1) the layout of the apartment did not meet their needs. As Magnusson Grossman stated, 'No architect should be allowed to design a kitchen without running a household for a couple of months! Please, keep us from the "rationalised" kitchens with all their expensive and fancy appliances but without decent cupboards for this and that.'[56] We cannot know whether Magnusson Grossman was familiar with Schütte-Lihotzky's designs for the Frankfurt Kitchen, but it is clear that she valued storage above efficiency, emphasising the kitchen as part of the larger domestic arena and not purely as a functional environment in which to store and prepare food. And from the same interview:

If I could wish for an ideal apartment, it would have spacious kitchen storage – without unnecessary floor space – and be without a hall, which usually is just a dark passage. The bedroom would be completely separated from the other rooms so you never would get smoke or noise there, and it would have a real room for the maid – not just an alcove, which is a nuisance – and beside the kitchen there would be a proper small room – not just a cramped box – for brushes, brooms, buckets, rags, detergents, a ladder, an ironing board, and such things. And naturally it would have beautiful and functional furniture in happy colours.[57]

Magnusson Grossman began testing these design principles in the Gärdet apartment. Although constrained by the dimensions of the footprint, her remodelling of its interior looked to open it up and establish a more porous relationship between domestic activities, with the living room as the focal point (Fig.30). In a 1941 interview with the *Los Angeles Times*, she states: 'The living-room is planned for three purposes: conversation, dining space, and desk or working space.'[58]

Throughout the apartment, the furniture was designed by Magnusson Grossman to perform a range of functions – the dining table, made of rosewood, extended to facilitate up to twelve guests and a side table accommodated the transfer of food from the kitchen. Here, as in her later homes, mirrors were used to great effect, offering unexpected vistas through the compact space, as well as reflecting daylight into it (Fig.31). The apartment also contained inherited objects from Magnusson Grossman's past, including a secretary's desk made by her great-grandfather and a 19th-century chest. Also noticeable is the use of colour to enrich and bring warmth to the space. Magnusson Grossman, although exposed to the austere white spaces of modernism during her European travels, did not mimic the starkness of these buildings and interiors. And, in a 1937 interview with *Svenska Hem*, Magnusson Grossman says: 'In a warmer climate, like in Switzerland or Italy, furniture of tubular steel is appropriate, because it has a chilling effect and stays cool. Thus white doesn't fit in our cold climate, where warmth indoors is absolutely necessary.'[59]

30　The Magnusson Grossmans' apartment in Gärdet, 1937. Photograph by Almberg and Preinitz

The layout of the Gärdet apartment and the design of the fixtures and fittings demonstrate Magnusson Grossman's early experiments in the *gesamtkunstwerk*, the 'total work of art'. Within the apartment, she was able to provide a meaningful context for her lamps, chairs and cabinets that relocates these objects away from the showroom and into an environment where they are transformed into animate devices that help to contrive the domestic mise-en-scène. Here, the desk lamp lights Magnusson Grossman at work, the bar facilitates social interaction and the soft furnishings bring comfort; although, as befitted the ideal functionalist interior, ease of cleaning and maintenance is key – the objects and spaces that Greta made for herself and her new husband to establish themselves 'at home' are alive and responsive to their needs.

AT HOME IN CALIFORNIA

The Magnusson Grossmans' move to California in 1940 offered new opportunities for Greta to develop her design practice, particularly in relation to the home. The atmosphere of this exciting and diverse environment would have been tremendously stimulating for a designer, with its delightful mix of cultures brought about by a significantly sized, resident refugee population. Magnusson Grossman herself recognised the value of this *milieu* – 'Now the best designers are here, the materials are here, and the casual, easy ways of living. The older countries have been horribly disrupted by war. It is up to this country to utilize the wealth of opportunities that today are hers.'[60]

The next house that Magnusson Grossman undertook to design for herself and Billy (on spec to sell on) was on Waynecrest Drive, completed in 1949 (Plate 7). This was her first chance to implement the architectural skills acquired at Sweden's KTH, Kungliga Tekniska Högskolan (Royal Institute of Technology).[61] In California, she collaborated with the engineer Ted Joehn in order to address the structural complexities of the site. With a steep slope on both sides, the location offered great views west and towards LA. The structure that Magnusson Grossman designed is cleverly positioned on the rocky terrain, perched above the ground and projecting outwards. The interior of the house is spread across different levels, navigating the topography of the site. These levels establish a fluid and permeable space that accommodates the different actions of everyday living and working. Rather than introducing walls into the interior to differentiate between activities, the changes in level offer a set of spaces that are separate but integrated (Plate 8). Waern suggests that the house at Waynecrest Drive references the turn-of-the-century Arts and Crafts architecture of Greene & Greene who practised largely in California, as well as the later Californian modernism of Richard Neutra – and it is certainly possible to detect elements of both practices in Magnusson Grossman's work.

The front facade of the house at Waynecrest Drive is 'closed' – a strategy that is repeated in other examples of Magnusson Grossman's architecture. Waern draws our attention to this feature in both the Nelson House from 1955 (Plate 11) and the Backus House from 1949–50 (Fig.32 and Plate 9), where the street-facing facade is closed off from traffic and the public gaze, while at the back the houses open onto the rocky Californian terrain. The glazing of the rear facades in these houses also utilises passive solar design – a sustainable strategy for heating buildings tested by the architect George Fred Keck in his 1930s 'solar houses'.[62] Another design trope that appears to characterise Magnusson Grossman's interiors is her use of large planters that establish permeable thresholds across spaces. It seems that this inclusion of plants within the domestic setting both link the interior to the landscape beyond as well as encourage what Magnusson Grossman described as 'our love of the open'.[63]

House Beautiful magazine described the Magnusson Grossmans' first home in Los Angeles as symbolic of 'a back-to-nature kind of Modern that sees sermons in stones and good in everything'.[64] Another article, written by Elsa Pehrson for *American Swedish Monthly*, goes further: 'Her own home provides a good cross-section of what is typical in her work. In it there is not a single piece of furniture, not a lamp, nor even such things as knives and forks, which she has not designed herself.'[65] Once again the

32   Exterior, Backus House, Bel Air Estates, Los Angeles, 1949–50. Photograph by Donald J. Higgins

idea of the 'total work of art' reveals itself in the design of Magnusson Grossman's own domestic environment. Yet we might also position her work within a history of sustainable architecture. Perhaps if Magnusson Grossman's approach to designing for the Californian climate had been recognised in her own time, critiques of modernism that focus on its wasteful use of concrete in particular – a material that requires constant maintenance – might have been swayed by Magnusson Grossman's sensitivity to context and to the re-use of artefacts which have yet to outlive their purpose.

Julius Schulman photographed the kitchen at Waynecrest Drive in 1949. The black and white image shows a functional space with timber built-in units that have ball cabinet handles – a motif

that can be seen later in her furniture for Glenn of California, and within the subsequent houses she designed. The breakfast bar is set for two, with what the R & Company exhibition catalogue from 2000 describes as 'traditional ceramics'.[66] The kitchen contains the obligatory spice rack on the wall – noted by Waern[67] to find its way into all of Magnusson Grossman's domestic interiors (Fig.33). Beyond the kitchen we catch a glimpse of the living space beyond, with a view to the LA hills. Although the photograph is uninhabited, it does capture a domestic scene that is comfortable and easy. The underlying philosophy of Magnusson Grossman's domestic architecture and in particular the spaces she designed for herself, extend and develop a functionalist narrative. Her choice

33   The Magnusson Grossmans' kitchen at Waynecrest Drive, Beverly Hills, 1948–49 (Note the spice rack, ball cabinet handles and string chairs). Photograph by Julius Shulman

of materials and use of colour bring warmth to the interior – even in the hot, sunny climate of LA, Magnusson Grossman is able to transpose the design language of her Nordic heritage to a location which would certainly have tolerated the austerity of continental modernism. Even though LA might well have provided the ideal conditions for the immaculate white and tubular steel of the Corbusian aesthetic, she recognised the appropriateness of a more humane modernity that works in harmony with its context, rather than resisting it.

According to Magnusson Grossman, 'to do a good job of planning, the designer must complete the entire design, from landscape and structure to furniture and decoration'.[68] This was to some extent at odds with what designer Alvin Lustig insisted made California different from Europe – 'its freedom from European tradition'.[69] Yet, what made Magnusson Grossman so successful was her ability to infuse modern design with the legacy of traditional Nordic aesthetics in a way that spoke of the future, not of the conflict-devastated past. Added to this was the advantage of the Californian climate, allowing a comfortable partitioning of indoor and outdoor domesticity. This was assisted by sliding glass doors, made possible by steel frame construction technologies developed during the Second World War. Californian design, declared Magnusson Grossman, 'is not a superimposed style, but an answer to present conditions . . . it has developed out of our own preference for living in a modern way.'[70]

The final home that Magnusson Grossman designed for herself and Billy was located at Claircrest Drive in Beverly Hills (Plates 13 and 14). Built between 1956 and 1957, the house sits lightly in the landscape, its elegant structure composed of two horizontal planar surfaces that frame the space between. This is a sophisticated piece of architecture that has reduced the structural elements to the bare minimum, while the interior enjoys endless flexibility through the creation of moveable, seven-foot walnut room dividers that change and adapt the space according to need or whim.

This is a house where the interior and exterior are fluid – moving glass panels slide away to create a continuous interior with free-standing

storage walls that can be reconfigured to create up to three bedrooms (Plate 15). The bathrooms have a fixed wall and are screened from the bedroom by low cabinets. There is also a fixed wall between the kitchen and the living space (Fig.34). As with other Magnusson Grossman-designed houses, there is a fireplace which operates as a focal point within the scheme. Usually identified as a device used by Frank Lloyd Wright in the design of his domestic interiors, the fireplace or hearth appears to epitomise the idea of home and homeliness. Rose Henderson's 1951 interview with Greta Magnusson Grossman and description of Claircrest Drive appears to be fascinated by the relationship between old and new evident in the home:

> Fitting perfectly into this streamlined interior is a huge old Swedish wooden chest, dating back through nobody-knows-how-many generations of Mrs Grossman's home-loving ancestors . . . And to the mistress of the house, it harks back to an intangible inheritance that must always be a vital part of her life. It seems to typify the hard-headed practicality and the simple, intrinsic beauty which characterize her work.[71]

At Claircrest Drive, the garden operates as a buffer zone between the house and the street. As with the rest of the house, this space is open to inhabitation and responsive to use. Photographs by John Hartley are virtually the only remaining document of this 'highly experimental'[72] interior and capture the lightness of the architecture, as well as the porous relationship between inside and out. There is a rather lovely image of Magnusson Grossman's workspace, given privacy from the living area by the placement of an elegant storage unit that seems to touch neither the floor nor the ceiling, but rather hovers in mid-air. Here is an early example of a live/work environment that situates work and domesticity in the same space. This lightness is also noted in Elsa Pehrson's 1944 article for the *American Swedish Monthly*: 'She has a talent for making an interior look light and aery, almost weightless. Even her heaviest pieces of furniture seem somehow to have lost their weight . . .'[73]

34   The kitchen at Claircrest Drive, with views over the valley, 1956–57

1951/2016

In 2016, Portuguese artist Leonor Antunes exhibited her Magnusson Grossman-inspired works at the San Francisco Museum of Modern Art. The exhibition brochure states: 'Leonor Antunes carries ghosts with her. Spirits of artists, designers, and architects she admires wander from exhibition to exhibition, object to object. Her sculptures capture glimpses of their histories, their lives, and their materials.'[74]

Antunes was captivated by an article in *Arts & Architecture*, published in 1951, that illustrates Magnusson Grossman's designs for a San Francisco residence. Familiar with the designer's name, but unaware that she had also designed houses, Antunes attempted to locate the residence depicted in the magazine, only to discover that it had never been built – in its place was an apartment block of uncertain heritage. In response to this absence of the anticipated dwelling, Antunes constructed her own version, working from measurements that she made on site. Jenny Gheith, the assistant curator at the museum, suggests that Antunes's 'measurements slip into the subjective realm of memory and time, falling closer to Marcel Duchamp's stoppages – conceptual gestures that captured the length of a meter through the chance driven curves of meter-long threads – than to a rational understanding of history'.[75]

Antunes' fascination with the lost work of Magnusson Grossman is captured in a number of the works exhibited and taps into what writer Stewart Brand has described as the 'shearing layers of change'[76] in a building, where the impact of inhabitation and use over time are resisted by the external building envelope. In *Backus House*, for example, Antunes looks to capture the modifications and discrepancies that exist between Magnusson Grossman's design for the residence and its 21st-century incarnation. Using measurements taken from the original drawings of the house and merging this with those made

35 *A spiral staircase leads down to the garden*, Leonor Antunes, 2016
Woven monofilament yarn, 159 × 8 × 8 in (403.9 × 20.3 × 20.3 cm)
(*New Work: Leonor Antunes*, San Francisco Museum of Modern Art)

36 *A skylight alley running sideways*, Leonor Antunes, 2016

Powder-coated brass plates, micro cable, stainless steel and brass beads (2 elements),
168 × 102 × 6 in (426.7 × 259.1 × 15.2 cm)
(*New Work: Leonor Antunes*, San Francisco Museum of Modern Art)

at the time of the artwork, Antunes articulates the shifts and changes that she found. In Figures 35 and 36 we can see how Antunes has mapped these discrepancies into the work *in situ*. The draped grey leather hangings that are suspended in the centre of the space and the cord that traces over the ceiling seem to capture the last traces of Magnusson Grossman's presence within Backus House – a building at risk from imminent erasure.

In all of these images of Antunes' work we can also see Magnusson Grossman's B-4 table lamp as a point of reference. Gubi, which has reissued the lamp along with other key pieces from Magnusson Grossman's portfolio of industrial design, suggests that the lamp most closely resembles her architecture, reflecting the way that her houses 'were perched high up on stilts with cantilevered decks and walls of glass to take in the magnificent hillside views'.[77] The moveable visors that also characterise the B-4 table lamp are captured in

A skylight alley running sideways. The art practice of Leonor Antunes offers a mirror to the history of 20th-century modernist design and reveals its absences and flaws.

Magnusson Grossman was not alone in her plight to be validated as a pioneer in her field. Art historian Magnus Olausson, in his analysis of Swedish design between the wars, returns to the idea that modernism itself is largely to blame.[78] Certainly the legacy of Magnusson Grossman has been thwarted by the repeated analogy between modernism and masculinity, and how history has tended to privilege the careers of architects and designers whose profiles fit this characterisation. But through the ongoing reclamation of Magnusson Grossman's significant catalogue of work via the archive, artistic endeavour and the reissuing of her furniture and lighting, or via textual analyses like this one, the status of her brand moving forward is increasingly promising.

4 Feminist Historiography: Reconstructing a Legacy

This book has set out to present the architecture and design of Greta Magnusson Grossman as a product of its time, but more significantly as a body of work that should be judged on its own merits and not simply in comparison to that of her peers. Here is a designer whose outputs have been overlooked, misattributed, misappropriated and more often ignored, but whose work has proved pivotal to the emergence of Californian design in the 1950–1960s and to mid-century modernism – genres whose development is otherwise almost exclusively attributed to men. In order to piece together the evidence base needed to substantiate this claim, we soon discovered that we would need to look beyond the historians – who had failed to fulfil their duty towards designer and discipline – to both industry and curators who specialise in constructing archives intended to increase the value and status of modernist furniture and lighting in the service of collectors. The format of these resources – more often articles from trade journals, artists' magazines and newspaper supplements – allegedly lack the integrity and objectivity of academic writing, calling into question the authority of our claims. But it is only through these sources that we can create the Trojan horse needed to mount an effective assault on the canon. This methodological approach draws inspiration and tactics from *archival activism*, a form of 'radical or counter-hegemonic history-making activity'[1] used as a means to offer a different perspective on what constitutes archival content, how it is classified and who gets to create it.

While Magnusson Grossman's story characterises what many women designers still expect from the design world and its academic associates, despite the passage of time, one does not need to identify as a woman or a feminist to understand the extent to which architecture's 'star system', with its adopted capitalist hierarchies, prefers to recognise and reward individuals. An instinctive collaborator such as Magnusson Grossman, who was deeply committed to working closely with her clients, would be deemed of lesser value within this system, where collective activities are largely overlooked. This issue resonates with architect and writer Denise Scott Brown's 1973 essay, 'Room at the Top: Sexism and the Star System in Architecture',[2] where she points to the undermining of women as a clear consequence of sexism in academia and the profession. The irony is that under the current system, whether women are workers within a large firm or 'stars' at the top of a practice, they are often not attributed with authorship of the work; their gender means that they lack a voice.[3]

Many magazine articles featuring Magnusson Grossman's work required her physical presence in the images in order to sell the products, and we notice this especially because few male architects were photographed 'at home' in their work. Although later photographs of Magnusson Grossman show her 'at work' in her home, the younger Magnusson Grossman is used repeatedly as a decorative object within the interiors she has designed. Similar to the autobiographical photography of Francesca Woodman – where her body is merged with the fabric of the house – Magnusson Grossman's objectification within her own work highlights a larger issue within our cultural milieu – that women have the same status as an artefact.

Retrospectively, within the context of post-Second World War California – and after collectivism became synonymous with global conflict – the selfish singularity of the detached, suburban, one-generation family house becomes what architect and writer George Wagner describes as 'both the test site and hothouse for fantasy projection' in his essay, 'The Lair of the Bachelor'.[4] Upon this stage, the role of each player is delineated around spaces for intentionally atomising activities: father in the study, the garage or basement recreation room with other men, mother in the kitchen and the children in the TV room 'glued to the set', all separated by stud-frame walls sheathed in hydrogen sulphide-seeping gypsum plasterboard and coated in carcinogenic lead paint.

For Magnusson Grossman, designing a space dedicated to a woman's professional identity and public independence within a domestic typology which, as we have discussed, is historically geared towards servitude and obscurity might be understood as an act of suffragism. To confront the assumption that the design of a domestic dwelling should focus exclusively upon the care and maintenance of others, and in particular the professional and public presence of the male husband, was, within this era, particularly radical. What we now take for granted – that a domestic space can provide women as well as men a space within which their professional and public presence can be incubated, nurtured and sustained – was, for Magnusson Grossman, at a prototype stage.

To argue for Magnusson Grossman is to argue for modernism as a democratising influence over traditional gender hierarchies. The extent to which modernism and women are mutually and similarly maligned is a subject explored elsewhere by one of the authors, within a paper that questions why James Bond's villains always live in modernist buildings, and why they – like Bond's women – end up being destroyed.[5] Ian Fleming's *Bond* series effectively dominated the cinema of the 1950s and 1960s, furthering the *Playboy politik* of the period within which Magnusson Grossman operated.

A few years before we began this project, Magnusson Grossman had been credited with co-founding the Californian Design Movement 'alongside her friend, Richard Neutra', but only in one recent account – 12 years after her death in 1999.[6] This recognition – significantly, accredited within a design magazine rather than an academic text – is only the tip of the iceberg. Magnusson Grossman's Barham Apartments on Barham Boulevard (Fig.37 and Plate 10) – built in 1950 and inventively perched upon and cantilevered over

37   Interior of the Barham Apartments, Barham Boulevard, Hollywood, Los Angeles, 1950. Photograph by Donald J. Higgins. At the time of writing the structure remains intact, but the apartments have been substantially remodelled

38   The Stahl House – Case
Study House 22, Pierre Koenig,
1959

an LA canyon – preceded Pierre Koenig's 1959
Case Study House 22 (Fig.38), also known as the
Stahl House, and brought to fame through the
photography of Julius Shulman in 1960. Yet only the
latter is credited with 'icon' status and celebrated
to date. Even today, the obvious appropriation is
ignored. That Shulman hired two women models
in cocktail dresses, rather than asking Koenig
to pose – in the way that Magnusson Grossman
was typically expected to within the spaces she
authored – further echoes the pervasiveness of
Playboy values at the time.

* * *

For our part, the humble aspiration is that this
book provides a methodology for finding inventive
ways to discover and share stories of forgotten
women designers that can be duplicated and
appropriated, and that can address our own

omissions in relation to Magnusson Grossman's
work or towards recovering other women designers'
narratives. There is an urgency here. Without an
acknowledgement within either the existing or the
decolonised canon discussed in the Introduction,
Magnusson Grossman's contribution towards
design and architecture remains undervalued –
exposing it to a lack of publications, resulting in a
lack of referencing and influence.

Magnusson Grossman's original furniture and
lighting have been largely ignored in retrospectives,
and until recently, collectors have been
uninterested in acquiring the originals. Are some
aspects of her absence from the canon a matter
of chance? It could be argued that Magnusson
Grossman's obscurity was, in part, due to her
choice of manufacturers – Glenn of California and
Ralph O. Smith, who later went bust, rather than
Herman Miller, who continues to this day and even
sells Magnusson Grossman's Grasshopper lamp.

41   View of the
open-plan kitchen
area, Villa Sundin,
Hudiksvall,
Sweden,
1959/2020

42   View of the
open-plan living
area, Villa Sundin,
Hudiksvall,
Sweden,
1959/2020

43   View of the
open-plan dining
area, Villa Sundin,
Hudiksvall,
Sweden,
1959/2020

The critical assumption here is that she chose her manufacturers, rather than the other way around. Still, Magnusson Grossman's lighting and furniture are experiencing a renaissance in the form of Gubi's edited re-release. Her architecture, however, is determinedly less well-known, and the remaining examples are at risk from demolition or substantial alteration. Without the acknowledgement of the canon, the houses that are left in LA and Sweden (Figs 39 to 43) remain unlisted, rendering them susceptible to demolition or alteration. The urgency is particularly acute in regard to the Hudiksvall House in Sweden, which she completed in 1959 and which retains many of its Magnusson Grossman interior elements, including furniture and fixtures.

As for the Californian houses, the original structures of both the Backus House (Figs 44, 45, 46) and the Nelson House (Figs 47 and 48; Plate 12)

illustrated here were intact ten years ago, but only the Nelson House is still standing – in 2020, the Backus House was demolished to make room for a new and larger dwelling.[7] California's laws have aggravated this situation. Tax rules governing the period in which the houses were built incentivised designers to build within a 1300 square foot (120 square metre) footprint and, as a consequence, restricted the scale of the homes. This impressed upon designers the need for space-saving efficiencies and, in Magnusson Grossman's case, she addressed this by using curtain walls of glass, extending the sense of space out into the views of the city below. Notwithstanding, the houses that remain are understood to be worth less than the land they sit upon. As a consequence, if they haven't been demolished, they are more than likely to have been extensively modernised, leaving little trace of Magnusson Grossman's

44   Exterior view from the west of Backus House, Bel Air Estates, Los Angeles, 1949–50. Photograph by Donald J. Higgins

45   Small dining area at Backus House, Bel Air Estates, Los Angeles, 1949–50

original design features intact. What is needed is some form of protection by historical societies or national landmark commissions, but this relies upon a better canonic imprint in order to make the case – the driver for writing this book in the first place. Further to this, the perceived value – both economic and cultural – of Magnusson Grossman's architecture, and interior design work in particular, is compromised by the metrics governing how historians typically identify, imprint and reference work deemed to possess architectural merit. Without material evidence, the means to position Magnusson Grossman in the canon is reduced, thus perpetuating the status quo. And if we, as feminist

archivists, fall short of destabilising the canon, then women will remain, as Beatriz Colomina posits, 'the ghosts of modern architecture, everywhere present, crucial, but strangely invisible. Unacknowledged, they are destined to haunt the field forever.'[8]

Magnusson Grossman's perceived lack of formal architectural qualifications has already been discussed, but it is pertinent here because this provides the benchmark that either legitimises her architecture or relegates it to the status of domestic artefact. Unless we acknowledge Magnusson Grossman as an architect as well as a designer, we are complicit

46   View of the upstairs deck with dining arrangement at Backus House,
Los Angeles, 1949–50. Photograph by Donald J. Higgins

47　Exterior view of the deck at Nelson House, Hollywood Knolls,
Los Angeles, 1955. Photograph by John Hartley

48   The Nelson House, Hollywood Knolls, Los Angeles, 1955.
Photograph by John Hartley

in reinforcing the perception that she merely played with making architecture, as if it were a hobby rather than her profession. As architects Eva Álvarez and Carlos Gómez point out in their 2017 *Architectural Review* article, 'The Invisible Women: How Female Architects Were Erased from History', authorship sits at the heart of this issue – within a highly competitive professional landscape which, as we have already seen, privileges the individual over the collective effort and from which women have been comprehensively erased.[9] However, we argue that there are three forms of authorship at stake: the creator, as in the architect; the canonic curator, encompassing historians and also journalists; and the consumer, that is, both the academics who organise reading lists and establish design precedents, and the students

who author their design projects and history assignments based upon these recommendations. This is precisely why authorship is a flawed tradition that has contributed to the oppression of women architects[10] and will continue to do so without some form of direct confrontation.

In 2014, Patty Hopkins, co-founder of Hopkins Architects, was controversially photoshopped out of an image with her husband Michael Hopkins during the promotion of a BBC documentary, *The Brits Who Built the Modern World*.[11] It is notable that the erased woman is married to the recognised man. This speaks to feminist and political scientist Jo Freeman's definition of sexism, described in her 1971 text, 'The Women's Liberation Movement: Its Origins, Structures and Ideas'. In it, Freeman states that, 'Sexism embodies two core concepts . . .': the first is 'that men do the important work in the world and the work done by men is what is important', while the second 'is that women's identities are defined by their relationship to men and their social value by that of the men they are related to'.[12] The legacy of women architects and designers is thus shaped within a scenario where both authorship and structural sexism impact on their past and present narratives.[13] Redressing this situation requires a deep interrogation of the ways in which architecture is produced. The erasure of Magnusson Grossman's authorship of her work across architectural and design history has distorted our understanding of mid-20th-century modernism, and it has contributed to the marginalisation of interior design as a legitimate profession within this narrative.

Magnusson Grossman did not publicly identify as a feminist, but that does not mean she did not operate as one. Feminism is both noun and adjective, and her pursuit of equality of both opportunity and reward afford her the title. Even in the 21st century, less than half of millennials identify as feminists,[14] despite benefiting directly from their historical efforts. However, taking the contraceptive pill, being paid equally at work, or choosing whom to love and whether to marry or not are all feminist acts. Consequently, to make architecture as a woman is an act of feminism. To expect the work to be equally valued could be described as feminist optimism. Or as Colomina contends, 'the previously marginal details of how things actually happen in architectural practice are now coming to light'.[15]

*   *   *

Although Magnusson Grossman's works were widely published in an array of significant publications – including the American *Arts & Architecture*, the French *Architecture d'Aujourd'hui* and the Italian *Domus* – it is largely thanks to the aforementioned John Entenza, editor in chief of *Arts & Architecture* between 1938 and 1962, that Magnusson Grossman's work was catalogued at all during this period. Entenza regularly featured her work, capturing aspects of her creative philosophy and personal life and laying the groundwork for a nascent theorisation of her contribution. Yet,

although we may applaud Entenza's recognition of Magnusson Grossman as a designer, as we highlighted earlier, he fell short of endorsing her as a potential contributor to the Case Study Houses programme, in which he was instrumental. Where other well-known (male) architects of the time were afforded the opportunity to establish their contribution to the modernist canon through their association with the programme, it feels as though Magnusson Grossman was overlooked.

The Case Study Houses programme – as it survives today through the architecture, photographs, design drawings, published ephemera and critical investigations devoted to it – serves as important archival documentation of Californian modernism. This material has simultaneously ensured the preservation of the built artefacts themselves, as well as the professional status of those who took part. All archives carry responsibility towards cultural products such as these, including their collection, cataloguing, preservation and distribution. And indeed, what qualifies as archival material within the decolonised canon is becoming more inclusive and diverse than ever before. Artists such as Zoe Beloff, whose work involves creating imagined archives with found materials of various origins, are able to confront and contest the very construction of an archive (Fig.49). Further to this, the materiality of the canon – moving beyond the major commission and the monograph, towards greater recognition of minor work, oral narratives and end-user testimonies – needs to be reconsidered, alongside the role of women as architecture investors, clients, design team members, lovers and muses.

As a designer who worked across disciplines, it has been contended that the career and legacy of Magnusson Grossman has perhaps suffered because of her breadth of interests and skills. The common criticism of a polymath is that, while they are able to turn their hand to any number of projects and demonstrate dexterity in a range of disciplines, they are perceived as a master, or indeed mistress, of none. That Magnusson Grossman gave up commercial design in order to pursue painting showed the ease with which her creativity could be redirected towards fulfilment in the face of frustration, and an ability to transpose

49   *DREAMLAND: The Coney Island Amateur Psychoanalytic Society and their Circle 1926–1972* installation, from 2009, by artist Zoe Beloff (Dolhuys Museum, Haarlem, the Netherlands)

her professional skills towards other processes and outputs. And yet this same trait is also held to account for her attributed failure to develop an expertise in any single facet of designing and making. This double standard is more keenly exposed when her polymathic outputs are compared to those of the established 'masters' of architecture – from Frank Lloyd Wright to Le Corbusier – who have been applauded for their diverse skill sets, including industrial design, textiles, vehicle design and even muralism. In contrast, Magnusson Grossman's disciplinary diversification and even hybridisation has been dismissed as a dilution of intention, as an indicator of a lack of focus or seriousness and, consequently, as a diminished body of work – insufficient in scale and substance to earn

the acknowledgement of any one of the three disciplinary canons to which she contributed.

Over the last 70 years, disciplinary fluidity has been a persistent problem for the interior designer struggling to establish a valid space within which to practise. The practice and theorisation of interior design has been – and continues to be – defined by its relationship to architecture, and not simply as *inside* architecture, but also *beneath* it and *to the side*. Interior design remains marginal and marginalised. For some feminists, this marginalisation is where true artistry or influence is situated. African-American, lesbian, feminist bell hooks, for example, discerned the position of marginality as the 'space of radical openness' and 'a site of creativity and power', as well as a 'space of resistance', in her writings.[16] Similarly, feminist architect Karen Franck questions what an interior design that 'elevated and celebrated' its marginal 'feminine' characteristics might look like – inviting designers to respond by focusing upon aspects of interiority that have been given low or no design attention whatsoever. Since the majority of the planet's population is female and that majority is systematically marginalised to ensure a few men succeed, then the margins are richly overpopulated by a community of remarkable women with the power and potential to look to each other, rather than the centre, in order to reimagine the value systems that created this binary. This resonates with what we have argued elsewhere: that the interior is 'resolutely dialogic and consistently collaborative . . . [it] fosters and encourages a mobile and expansive discourse that is able to plug into a variety of disciplines, creating and exploiting networks of communication across them'.[17]

To conclude, we see little changing for women within the design disciplines without strategic and fundamentally feminist action, as it is only the sacrifices – as much as the successes – of feminism that have enabled us to make this claim in the first place. However, what closer scrutiny of the Magnusson Grossman story has taught us is that there is no criterion that can be offered for feminist archivists other than to trust in and value the subjectivity of their own approach. Design books, whether academically oriented or intended as a 'coffee-table read', need to be written by new voices and to explore new ways of capturing, cataloguing and critiquing the material in order for such books to reach new audiences. We recognise that our methodological tactics are not inventive, but merely innovative – an adaptation and appropriation of an amalgamation of approaches intended to better define the nature of the problem than able to provide an original solution. However, they are necessary prototypes, whose weaknesses provide a means through which a true invention can occur. And when it does, we would encourage the next generation to revisit Magnusson Grossman and critically appraise this text for its failure to achieve this –

in light of the methods they will then know to be both worthy and more effective.

* * *

When we began researching this book, we already understood that Greta Magnusson Grossman was a designer who had been largely omitted from the canon of modern architecture, interior design and industrial design. As a polymath – who was prolific within the field first in Stockholm and later in California – it nevertheless seemed strange that she had failed to penetrate the public consciousness. Furthermore, as students of the subject in the late 20th century, neither of us were ever exposed to her work or came across her in the process of shaping our individual design practices.

Magnusson Grossman's career as a designer was fundamentally centred on the interior as the primary milieu for her work. Creating furniture, lighting and textiles for both showrooms and the home, her work establishes a mode of inhabitation that demonstrates a strong sensibility for the rituals of daily life. The houses that Magnusson Grossman designed for herself and her clients in California and Sweden further reflect the changing relationship between home and work as overlapping spheres, rather than separate and independent from one another. Magnusson Grossman also allowed the surrounding landscape to shape the architecture by designing structures that were modest in scale and sit lightly on their plot. Like the Case Study Houses, these homes experimented with light and materials, and tested the organisation and hierarchies of domestic space.

Evidently, it is Magnusson Grossman's successes as well as her sacrifices that have made this book possible. Her talent. Her determination in the face of unilateral disadvantage. Her bravery in stepping up and stepping down. The injustice of her exclusion and obscurity. Consequently, it is to her that we owe, in part, our awareness of the issues, our presence within this discourse, and our entitlement to equality – and a voice of our own – within our disciplines.

Afterword: Archival Activism

In the summer of 2020 we commissioned two photographers based in LA to locate and document what remains of Magnusson Grossman's California houses. We had originally intended to undertake this piece of detective work ourselves, but the restrictions brought about by the global pandemic prevented us from making this 'pilgrimage' to view the remains and mourn what has been lost. The photographers' investigations revealed the recent demolition of the Backus House and extensive modifications to other properties. Happily, the Nelson House, both upper and lower, is largely intact, and photographs taken of the interiors depict aspects of Magnusson Grossman's original fixtures and fittings, including the fireplace. We also requested that the photographers scan the houses, where permission was given, in order to evidence and preserve the architecture in lieu of its potential disappearance. This technology has the capacity to expose layers of hidden data and to produce a photographic image that brings to the surface the lost traces of previous iterations and interactions – in this instance allowing us to document key aspects of Magnusson Grossman's designs for a future audience. The resulting photogrammetry is strangely haunting – like an echo across time, it captures something almost visceral; we feel the architecture inside ourselves almost as if we were present at the time of its inception.

top

53   Exterior view, Upper Nelson House
from the street, 1955/2020

bottom

54   Photogrammetry of the exterior,
Upper Nelson House, 1955/2020

left, main photograph

50   Exterior view, Nelson House
from the street, 1955/2020

bottom left

51   Photogrammetry of the exterior,
Nelson House, 1955/2020

bottom right

52   Photogrammetry of the interior,
Nelson House, 1955/2020

55 View of the dining area, Upper Nelson House showing the fireplace, 1955/2020

56 Interior view, Upper Nelson House, 1955/2020

57   Exterior view from the street of Waynecrest Drive, 1948–49/2020

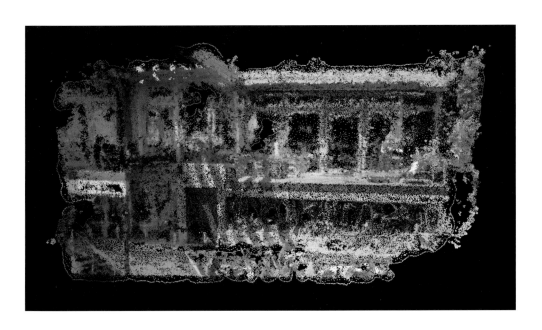

58   Photogrammetry of the valley view of Waynecrest Drive, 1948–49/2020

left

59   View of the fireplace at
Waynecrest Drive, 1948–49/2020

below

60   Photogrammetry of the main
living space at Waynecrest Drive,
1948–49/2020

Notes

FOREWORD

1   A traditional Scandinavian mulled wine.
2   As described by Frank Harris and Weston David Bonenberger, *A Guide to Contemporary Architecture in Southern California* (Los Angeles: Watling, 1951).

INTRODUCTION

1   Greta Magnusson Grossman, quoted in Rose Henderson, 'A Swedish Furniture Designer in America: An Interview with Greta Magnusson Grossman', *American Artist*, no.150, December 1951, p.56.
2   Harriet Harriss and Naomi House, 'Interiority Complex', in James Benedict Brown, Harriet Harriss, Ruth Morrow and James Soane (eds), *A Gendered Profession: The Question of Representation in Space Making* (London: RIBA Books, 2016).
3   Arianna Schioldager, 'Greta Magnusson Grossman: Walking Away', *Art Papers*, vol.37, no.2, 2013, p.39.
4   Lily Kane, *Greta Magnusson Grossman: Designer* (New York: R Gallery, 2000), p.12.
5   Jane Jacobs, cited in Carmen Espegel, 'Women and Architecture', in *Women Architects in the Modern Movement* (Abingdon: Routledge, 2018), p.23.
6   Carmen Espegel, 'Part 3 – Two X Chromosomes in Modern Architecture', in ibid.
7   Gurminder K. Bhambra, Kerem Nişancioğlu and Dalia Gebrial (eds), *Decolonising the University* (London: Pluto Press, 2018), p.34.
8   Nelson Maldonado-Torres, 'Thinking through the Decolonial Turn: Post-continental Interventions in Theory, Philosophy, and Critique – An Introduction', *Transmodernity: Journal of Peripheral Cultural Production of the Luso-Hispanic World*, vol.1, no.2, 2011.
9   Anne Sisson Runyan, 'Decolonizing Knowledges in Feminist World Politics', *International Feminist Journal of Politics*, vol.20, no.1, 2018, pp 3–8. Available at https://www.tandfonline.com/doi/full/10.1080/14616742.2018.1414403. Accessed 26 June 2020.
10   Chandra Talpade Mohanty, 'Transnational Feminist Crossings: On Neoliberalism and Radical Critique', *Signs: Journal of Women in Culture and Society*, vol.38, no. 4, 2013, pp 967–91.
11   Susana Torre, 'Feminism and Architecture, Part 1: Feminist Contributions', 21 August 2014. Available at https://archiparlour.org/feminism-and-architecture-part-1-the-contribution-of-feminism/. Accessed 21 July 2019.
12   Nils G. Wollin, cited in Gillian Naylor, 'Swedish Grace . . . or the Acceptable Face of Modernism?', in Paul Greenhalgh (ed.), *Modernism in Design* (London: Reaktion Books, 1990), p.164.
13   J.M. Richards, cited in ibid., p.165.
14   Tim Abrahams, 'Swedish Modern', *Blueprint*, no.307, October 2011, p.66.
15   Suneet Zishan Langar, '9 Incredibly Famous Architects Who Didn't Possess an Architecture Degree', *ArchDaily*, 19 June 2017. Available at https://www.archdaily.com/873850/9-incredibly-famous-architects-who-didnt-possess-an-architecture-degree. Accessed 26 June 2020.
16   Abrahams, op.cit., pp 66–7.
17   Henderson, op.cit., p.56.
18   Abrahams, op.cit., p.66.
19   ibid., p.68.
20   Mary McLeod, 'Everyday and "Other" Spaces', in Debra Coleman, Elizabeth Danze and Carol Henderson (eds), *Architecture and Feminism* (New York: Princeton Architectural Press, 1996), p.20.
21   Evan Snyderman, 'Introduction', in Andrea Codrington, *Greta Magnusson Grossman – A Car and Some Shorts: One Architect's Journey from Sweden to Southern California* (Stockholm: Arkitekturmuseet, 2010), p.11.
22   ibid., p.67.
23   'Good Design Is Appearance Plus Comfort: Swedish-born Designer Works Toward the Perfect Combination', *Western Upholstery Furniture & Bedding*, April 1953, p.7.
24   Schioldager, op.cit., p.36.
25   ibid., p.36.
26   ibid., p.38.
27   ibid., p.40.

1   SWEDISH ORIGINS

1   Carmen Espegel, *Women Architects in the Modern Movement* (Abingdon: Routledge, 2018), p.10.
2   Ellen Key, cited in Andrea Codrington, *Greta Magnusson Grossman – A Car and Some Shorts: One Architect's Journey from Sweden to Southern California* (Stockholm: Arkitekturmuseet, 2010), p.20.

3   Codrington, ibid., p.17.
4   ibid., p.17.
5   Greta Magnusson Grossman, quoted in 'Up and coming: Five whose stars are shining in the design world', *House & Garden*, June 1947, pp 30–39.
6   Anne-Marie Bohlin, cited in Codrington, op.cit., p.18.
7   Cited in ibid., p.19.
8   Cilla Robach, 'Design for Modern People', in Cecilia Widenheim (ed.), *Utopia and Reality: Modernity in Sweden 1900–1960* (New Haven: Yale University Press, 2002), p.188.
9   Codrington, op.cit., p.19.
10   ibid., p.19.
11   ibid., p.19.
12   Greta Magnusson Grossman, cited in ibid., p.20.
13   Ralph Alton, cited in ibid., p.22.
14   Gillian Naylor, 'Swedish Grace . . . or the Acceptable Face of Modernism?', in Paul Greenhalgh (ed.), *Modernism in Design* (London: Reaktion Books, 1990), p.172.
15   ibid., p.172.
16   ibid., p.173.
17   ibid., p.174.
18   Hermann Muthesius, cited in ibid., p.167.
19   ibid.
20   Le Corbusier, cited in Victor Arwas, *Art Deco* (New York: Abrams Books, 1992), p.46.
21   Uno Åhrén, cited in Lasse Brunnström, *Swedish Design: A History* (London: Bloomsbury, 2018), p.56.
22   P. Morton Shand, cited in Naylor, op.cit., p.171.
23   Uno Åhrén, cited in Robach, op.cit., p.193.
24   Brunnström, op.cit., p.4.
25   ibid., p.63.
26   Ingeborg Glambek, cited in ibid., p.55.
27   J.M. Richards, cited in Naylor, op.cit., p.179.
28   Codrington, op.cit., p.25.
29   Greta Magnusson Grossman, cited in ibid., p.26.
30   Eva Rudberg, 'Utopia of the Everyday', in Cecilia Widenheim (ed.), *Utopia and Reality: Modernity in Sweden 1900–1960* (New Haven and London: Yale University Press, 2002), p.153.
31   ibid., p.153.
32   Kenneth Frampton, 'The Untimely Timeliness of Swedish Modernism', in Lucy Creagh, Helena Kåberg and Barbara Miller Lane (eds), *Modern Swedish Design: Three Founding Texts* (New York: Museum of Modern Art, 2008), p.16.
33   *Sydsvenska Dagbladet*, cited in Rudberg, op.cit., p.155.
34   Morton Shand, cited in Naylor, op.cit., p.164.
35   Nicholas Bullock, 'Review of *The Stockholm Exhibition 1930: Modernism's Breakthrough in Swedish Architecture* by Eva Rudberg', *Architectural Research Quarterly*, vol.4, no.1, March 2000, p.90.

Available at https://www.cambridge.org/core/journals/arq-architectural-research-quarterly/article/stockholm-exhibition-1930-modernisms-breakthrough-in-swedish-architecture-by-eva-rudberg-stockholmia-forlag-stockholm-1999238-pp-c190-mono-and-c65-colour-illus-isbn-9170310912-price-sek-352/DCB86AC0BB9588B5614159D1EF97B4C7#r. Accessed 15 April 2019.
36   Rudberg, op.cit., p.155.
37   Creagh, Kåberg and Miller Lane (eds), op.cit., pp 130, 341.
38   Rudberg, op.cit., p.159.
39   Codrington, op.cit., p.22.
40   Naylor, op.cit., p.177.
41   Morton Shand, cited in Naylor, ibid., p.177.
42   Brunnström, op.cit., p.59.
43   ibid., p.60.
44   Richards, cited in Naylor, op.cit., p.179.
45   Codrington, op.cit., p.20.
46   Gregor Paulsson, cited in Brunnström, op.cit., p.47.
47   Paulsson, cited in Naylor, op.cit., p.170.
48   ibid., p.170.
49   Creagh, Kåberg and Miller Lane (eds), op.cit., p.11.
50   Ellen Key, cited in ibid., p.11.
51   Frampton, op. cit, p.15.
52   Rudberg, op.cit., p.154.
53   ibid., p.154.
54   Robach, op.cit., p.197.
55   Brunnström, op.cit., p.65.
56   ibid., p.80.
57   ibid., p.69.
58   ibid., p.69.
59   Robach, op.cit., p.199.
60   ibid., p.199.
61   Magnusson Grossman was awarded a travel grant to supplement her Konstfack education, Codrington, op.cit., p.23.
62   Greta Magnusson Grossman, cited in ibid., p.24.
63   *Nya Dagligt Allehanda*, cited in ibid., p.25.
64   Codrington, ibid., p.25.
65   ibid., p.25.
66   ibid., p.23.
67   *Nya Dagligt Allehanda*, cited in ibid., p.27.
68   Greta Magnusson Grossman, cited in ibid., p.27.
69   ibid., p.27.
70   ibid., p.27.
71   Codrington, ibid., p.29.
72   Cited in ibid., p.29.
73   Codrington, ibid., p.50.
74   ibid., p.53.
75   *Stockholms-Tidningen*, cited in ibid., p.52.
76   *Dagens Nyheter*, cited in ibid., p.53.
77   Robach, op.cit., pp 193–4.
78   Codrington, op.cit., p.54.
79   ibid., p.54.

80 Åke Stavenow, cited in Eva Storgaard, 'Curating the Collective House: The Popularisation of a New Housing Model in 1930s Sweden', in Gaia Caramellino and Stéphanie Dadour (eds), *The Housing Project: Discourse, Ideals, Models and Politics in 20th Century Exhibitions* (Leuven: Leuven University Press, 2020), p.52.

81 Codrington, op.cit., p.55.

82 Talbot Hamlin, cited in ibid., p.55.

83 Cited in ibid., pp 55–6.

84 Gunnar Åselius, *The Rise and Fall of the Soviet Navy in the Baltic, 1921–1941* (Abingdon: Routledge, 2005), p.166.

2   A WELL-KNOWN DESIGNER

1 'New Career Sought: Couple Arrive from Sweden', *The San Francisco Examiner*, 27 July 1940.

2 'Good Design Is Appearance Plus Comfort: Swedish-born Designer Works Toward the Perfect Combination', *Western Upholstery Furniture & Bedding*, April 1953, p.7.

3 Andrea Codrington, *Greta Magnusson Grossman – A Car and Some Shorts: One Architect's Journey from Sweden to Southern California* (Stockholm: Arkitekturmuseet, 2010), p.57.

4 'Swedish Designer to Work on West Coast', *Retailing*, 4 November 1940.

5 Codrington, op.cit., p.58.

6 Greta Magnusson Grossman, cited in ibid.

7 Bettye Reeder, *Beverly Hills Citizen*, December 1941.

8 Arthur Miller, 'Art Parade Reviewed', *Los Angeles Times*, 9 March 1941, p.8.

9 Codrington, op.cit., p.60.

10 Dolores Barracano Schmidt, 'The Great American Bitch', *College English*, vol.32, no.8, 1971, p.900.

11 Bruce Brooks Pfeiffer and Frank Lloyd Wright, *Treasures of Taliesin: Seventy-seven Unbuilt Designs* (Portland: Pomegranate, 1999), p.58.

12 Codrington, op.cit., p.61.

13 ibid., p.9.

14 'Swedish Modern', *Designs* (Rehearsal Issue), August 1947, p.9.

15 Greta Magnusson Grossman, quoted in Rose Henderson, 'A Swedish Furniture Designer in America: An Interview with Greta Magnusson Grossman', *American Artist*, no.150, December 1951, p.56.

16 Erin Leary, '"The Total Absence of Foreign Subjects": The Racial Politics of US Interwar Exhibitions of Scandinavian Design', *Design and Culture*, vol.7, no.3, 2015, pp 283–312.

17 Bruce Brooks Pfeiffer and Frank Lloyd Wright, *Frank Lloyd Wright, 1867–1959: Building for Democracy* (Cologne: Taschen, 2004).

18 Katie Richards, 'Ikea's Top Designer on the Gift of Failure and the Future of Democratic Design: Marcus Engman Says Ikea is More than Just a Brand', *Adweek*, 25 May 2017. Available at https://www.adweek.com/creativity/ikeas-top-designer-on-the-gift-of-failure-and-the-future-of-democratic-design/. Accessed 26 June 2020.

19 Pamela Danziger, 'Ikea Realizes Democratic Design for the Home', *Forbes*, 12 June 2018. Available at https://www.forbes.com/sites/pamdanziger/2018/06/12/ikea-realizes-democratic-design-for-the-home/#4e1433f1469e. Accessed 26 June 2020.

20 Hans Krondahl, 'Tema Lunning Prize Winners', *Runeberg*. Retrieved 3 January 2018. Also see http://danishdesignreview.com/the-lunning-prize.

21 Widar Halén and Kerstin Wickman (eds), *Scandinavian Design Beyond the Myth: Fifty Years of Scandinavian Design from the Nordic Countries* (Stockholm: Arvinius, 2003).

22 Magnus Englund and Chrystina Schmidt, *Scandinavian Modern* (London: Ryland Peters & Small, 2007).

23 Codrington op.cit., p.98.

24 'New Furniture by Greta Grossman for Barker Brothers', *Arts & Architecture*, no.7, July 1947, p.32.

25 Codrington, op.cit., p.98.

26 'Up and Coming: Five Whose Stars are Shining in the Design World', *House & Garden*, June 1947.

27 'Barker Brothers Remodels Modern Floor', *Upholstering*, November 1947.

28 'Retail Trade: The Los Angeles Spirit', *Time*, 1 January 1945. Available at http://content.time.com/time/magazine/article/0,9171,791859,00.html. Accessed 4 August 2020.

29 Lily Kane, *Greta Magnusson Grossman: Designer* (New York: R Gallery, 2000), p.16.

30 'Acres of Modern Opened at Barker Bros., Los Angeles', *Retailing Home Furnishings*, 8 May 1947.

31 Kane, op.cit., pp 18–19.

32 Codrington, op.cit., p.11.

33 Wendy Kaplan (ed.), *California Design, 1930–1965: Living in a Modern Way* (Cambridge, MA: MIT Press and Los Angeles County Museum of Art, 2011), p.45.

34 In an example of everyday sexism, when not directly stated, this was the default inference of the singular emphasis on the housewife as a 'superior mother' – in just one of myriad examples; Ernst Dichter, cited in Ellen Lupton, *Mechanical Brides: Women and Machines from Home to Office* (New York: Cooper-Hewitt, National Museum of Design, Smithsonian Institution; Princeton, NJ: Princeton Architectural Press, 1993), p.10.

35 Elza Schallert, 'A Noted Architect Speaks – Simplicity in Home Design Called Keynote to Family Preservation', *Los Angeles Times*, 8 July 1954, p.B2.

36 Codrington, op.cit., p.13.

37   Taken from an unnamed clip in Magnusson Grossman's press book, and recounted in Codrington, ibid., p.59.

38   Elsa Pehrson, 'West Coast Designer', *American Swedish Monthly*, October 1944.

39   Arianna Schioldager, 'Greta Magnusson Grossman: Walking Away', *Art Papers*, vol.37, no.2, 2013, p.38.

40   Pehrson, op.cit.

41   Codrington, op.cit., p.99.

42   Greta Magnusson Grossman, quoted in Henderson, op.cit., pp 54–7.

43   Janet McHendrie, 'Smart Ways to Save Space', *Los Angeles Times*, 17 July 1949, p.8, cited in Codrington, op.cit., p.100.

44   Elizabeth Gordon, 'The New American Look', *House Beautiful*, March 1949, pp 118–24.

45   Greta Magnusson Grossman, quoted in Henderson, op.cit., pp 54–7.

46   Sam Hall Kaplan and Julius Shulman, *LA Lost & Found: An Architectural History of Los Angeles* (Santa Monica, CA: Hennessey and Ingalls, 2000), p.129.

47   ibid., p.129.

48   ibid., p.56.

49   Richard Neutra, quoted in ibid., p.147.

50   Edward P. Eichler, *Race and Housing: An Interview with Edward P. Eichler, President, Eichler Homes Inc.* (Santa Barbara: Fund for the Republic, 1964), p.19.

51   Reyner Banham, *Los Angeles: The Architecture of Four Ecologies* (Oakland: University of California Press, 2009), p.225.

52   Garrett Eckbo, *Landscape for Living* (Amherst, MA: University of Massachusetts Press, 1950).

53   Kaplan and Shulman, op.cit., p.127.

54   Schallert, op.cit.

55   Letter to Magnusson Grossman from Shelby B. Smith, Chief, Photo Facilities Section, Photographic branch of the International Press and Publications Division, 5 February 1952.

56   Henderson, op.cit.

57   *Western Upholstery Furniture & Bedding*, op.cit.

58   Codrington, op.cit., p.32.

59   *Good Design*, Museum of Modern Art, New York, 1952, exh.cat.

60   Kaplan and Shulman, op.cit., p.101.

61   Jacob Gubi, interview with Harriet Harriss, 21 August 2018.

62   ibid.

63   Codrington, op.cit., pp 106–7.

64   'Greta Grossman'. Available at https://www.laconservancy.org/architects/greta-grossman. Accessed 21 July 2019.

65   Greta Magnusson Grossman, quoted in Jean Krenzner, 'New Directions', *Los Angeles Times*, 5 June 1960, p.N27.

66   ibid., p.N27.

67   Codrington, op.cit., pp 108–9.

68   Greta Magnusson Grossman interview by Sigrid Eklund, c.1988, cited in ibid., p.103.

3   LIVING IN A MODERN WAY

1   Grace Lees-Maffei, 'Introduction: Professionalization as a Focus in Interior Design History', *Journal of Design History*, vol.21, no.1, Spring 2008, p.1. Available at https://doi.org/10.1093/jdh/epn007. Accessed 19 August 2019.

2   Charles Rice, *The Emergence of the Interior: Architecture, Modernity, Domesticity* (Abingdon: Routledge, 2007), p.4.

3   Adrian Scott Fine, of the Los Angeles Conservancy, quoted in Jen Carson, 'A Brief History of the Iconic Bungalows of LA', *LAist*, 15 April 2016. Available at https://laist.com/2016/04/15/bungalow_history.php. Accessed 19 August 2019.

4   George Wagner, 'The Lair of the Bachelor', in Debra Coleman, Elizabeth Danze and Carol Henderson (eds), *Architecture and Feminism* (New York: Princeton Architectural Press, 1996), p.185.

5   ibid., p.187.

6   ibid., p.195.

7   Gail Dines, Bob Jensen and Ann Russo, *Pornography: The Production and Consumption of Inequality* (Abingdon: Routledge, 2013), p.43.

8   *Playboy*, 1953, no.1, p.16.

9   Phillip Wylie, 'The Womanization of America', *Playboy*, 1958, p.78.

10   Reed, cited in Rice, op.cit., p.107.

11   Rice, ibid., p.107.

12   Phineas Harper, 'The Vision of the Home as a Tranquil Respite from Labour Is a Patriarchal Fantasy', *Dezeen*, 18 April 2019. Available at https://www.dezeen.com/2019/04/18/nuclear-family-home-tool-repression-phineas-harper/?utm_medium=email&utm_campaign=Daily%20Dezeen&utm_content=Daily%20Dezeen+CID_077e49a9ee188e47042f3f8c479374f6&utm_source=Dezeen%20Mail&utm_term=The%20vision%20of%20the%20home%20as%20a%20tranquil%20respite%20from%20labour%20is%20a%20patriarchal%20fantasy. Accessed 26 June 2020.

13   ibid.

14   Pier Vittorio Aureli and Maria Shéhérazade Giudici, 'Familiar Horror: Toward a Critique of Domestic Space', cited in ibid.

15   While attributed to Homi K. Bhabha (2000), Edward W. Soja has explored the term from a critical urban theory perspective – in just one example: *Thirdspace: Journeys to Los Angeles and Other Real-and-Imagined Places* (Oxford: Basil Blackwell, 1996).

16   Arnault Morrison, 'A Typology of Places in the Knowledge Economy: Towards the Fourth Place', in Francesco Calabrò, Lucia Della Spina and Carmelina Bevilacqua (eds), *New Metropolitan Perspectives*, Smart Innovation, Systems and Technologies, vol.100 (Cham: Springer, 2018).

17   ibid.

18   Terence Riley, cited in Rice, op.cit., p.114.

19   Karin Åberg Waern, 'Modern Living', in Andrea Codrington, *Greta Magnusson Grossman – A Car and Some Shorts: One Architect's Journey from Sweden to Southern California* (Stockholm: Arkitekturmuseet, 2010), p.131.

20   ibid.

21   Elsa Pehrson, 'West Coast Designer', *American Swedish Monthly*, October 1944, p.12.

22   ibid., p.11.

23   Rice, op.cit., p.2.

24   Penny Sparke, cited in Lees-Maffei, op.cit., p.8.

25   Originally coined in Italian; the slogan 'dal cucchiaio alla città' [from the spoon to the city] was intended to establish continuity in the built environment down to the tiniest detail in designed objects. Ernesto Rogers was, amongst other roles, editor of *Casabella*, 1953–1964, then temporarily branded *Casabella-Continuità*.

26   Sparke, cited in Lees-Maffei, op.cit., p.4.

27   Penny Sparke, 'The Designed Interior', in *The Modern Interior* (London: Reaktion Books, 2008), p.191.

28   Pat Kirkham, 'Humanizing Modernism: The Crafts, "Functioning Decoration" and the Eameses', *Journal of Design History*, vol.11, no.1, 'Craft, Modernism and Modernity', 1998, p.21.

29   Sparke, 'The Designed Interior', op.cit., p.186.

30   ibid., p.188.

31   ibid., p.188.

32   Eliot Noyes, *Organic Design in Home Furnishings*, exh.cat., MoMA, 1941. Available at https://www.moma.org/calendar/exhibitions/1803. Accessed 18 July 2019.

33   Mary Davis Gillies, cited in Sparke, 'The Designed Interior', op.cit., p.196.

34   George Nelson, cited in Sparke, ibid., pp 194–5.

35   Rice, op.cit., pp 102–3.

36   ibid., p.83.

37   ibid., p.99.

38   Le Corbusier, cited in ibid., p.104.

39   Beatriz Colomina, cited in ibid., p.104.

40   Esther McCoy, from the introduction to a monograph on the Case Study Houses programme, cited in Sam Hall Kaplan and Julius Shulman, *LA Lost & Found: An Architectural History of Los Angeles* (Santa Monica, CA: Hennessey and Ingalls, 2000), p.133.

41   Alexandra Griffith Winton, '"A Man's House Is His Art": The Walker Art Center's *Idea House* Project and the Marketing of Domestic Design 1941–1947', *Journal of Design History*, vol.17, no.4, 2004, p.378.

42   Beatriz Colomina, cited in ibid., p.379.

43   Lily Kane, *Greta Magnusson Grossman: Designer* (New York: R Gallery, 2000), p.12. See bibliography for many of the Swedish newspaper and magazine articles that document this period.

44   Greta Magnusson Grossman, quoted in ibid.

45   Karen A. Franck, 'A Feminist Approach to Architecture: Acknowledging Women's Ways of Knowing', in Ellen Perry Berkeley and Matilda McQuaid (eds), *Architecture: A Place for Women* (Washington, DC: Smithsonian Institution Press, 1989).

46   Lucinda Kaukas Havenhand, 'A View from the Margin: Interior Design', *Design Issues*, vol.20, no.4, p.39. Available at https://www.mitpressjournals.org/doi/10.1162/0747936042312002. Accessed 19 August 2019.

47   Harriet Harriss and Naomi House, 'Interiority Complex', in James Benedict Brown, Harriet Harriss, Ruth Morrow and James Soane (eds), *A Gendered Profession: The Question of Representation in Space Making* (London: RIBA Books, 2016), p.210.

48   'A Brief History of the Workhome'. Available at http://www.theworkhome.com/history-workhome/. Accessed 26 June 2020.

49   Greta Magnusson Grossman, quoted in Rose Henderson, 'A Swedish Furniture Designer in America: An Interview with Greta Magnusson Grossman', *American Artist*, no.150, December 1951, p.56.

50   Greta Magnusson Grossman, quoted in Elza Schallert, 'A Noted Architect Speaks – Simplicity in Home Design Called Keynote to Family Preservation', *Los Angeles Times*, 8 July 1954, p.2.

51   Kirkham, op.cit., p.27.

52   Charles and Ray Eames, cited in Kirkham, ibid., p.25.

53   Kirkham, ibid., p.27.

54   Greta Magnusson Grossman, quoted in Henderson, op.cit., p.56.

55   Waern, op.cit., p.131.

56   Greta Magnusson Grossman, quoted in Waern, p.131.

57   ibid.

58   Greta Magnusson Grossman, quoted in 'Home Furnishing Art Ranks High in Sweden', *Los Angeles Times*, 24 September 1941, p. B10.

59   Greta Magnusson Grossman, quoted in Waern, op.cit., p.132.

60   ibid., p.133.

61   ibid., p.133.

62   ibid., p.134.

63   Greta Magnusson Grossman, quoted in ibid., p.135.

64   'Some Modern Is Nothing but Unpretentious-ness', *House Beautiful*, March 1943, p.26.

65   Pehrson, op.cit., p.12.

66   R & Company, cited in Kane, op.cit., p.36.

67   Waern, op.cit., p.135.

68   'Good Design Is Appearance Plus Comfort: Swedish-born Designer Works Toward the Perfect Combination', *Western Upholstery Furniture & Bedding*, April 1953, p.7.

69   Alvin Lustig, 'Californian Modern', *Designs*, October 1947, pp 7–10.

70   Greta Magnusson Grossman, quoted in Henderson, op. cit., p.56.

71   Henderson, ibid.

72   Waern, op.cit., pp 136–7.

73   Pehrson, op.cit., p.12.

74   Jenny Gheith, *New Work: Leonor Antunes Brochure*, San Francisco Museum of Modern Art, 2016, p.2.

75   ibid., p.3.

76   This concept was outlined in his book, Stewart Brand, *How Buildings Learn: What Happens After They're Built* (New York: Viking, 1994).

77   B-4 table lamp on Gubi website. Available at https://shop.gubi.com/products/b-4-table-lamp?variant=31699690029196. Accessed 4 August 2020.

78   Magnus Olausson, 'Women Pioneers: Swedish Design In Between the Wars', *Art Bulletin of Nationalmuseum Stockholm*, vol.22, 2015, p.164. Available at http://www.diva-portal.org/smash/get/diva2:998770/FULLTEXT02. Accessed 19 August 2019.

4   FEMINIST HISTORIOGRAPHY: RECONSTRUCTING A LEGACY

1   Andrew Flinn, 'Archival Activism: Independent and Community-led Archives, Radical Public History and the Heritage Professions', *InterActions: UCLA Journal of Education and Information Studies*, vol.7, no.2, 2011. Available at http://escholarship.org/uc/item/9pt2490x.

2   Denise Scott Brown, 'Room at the Top: Sexism and the Star System in Architecture', *Architectural Design*, vol.60, nos 1–2 (1990), U1–U2.

3   Eva Álvarez and Carlo Gómez, 'The Invisible Women: How Female Architects Were Erased from History', *The Architectural Review*, 8 March 2017. Available at https://www.architectural-review.com/essays/the-invisible-women-how-female-architects-were-erased-from-history/10017481.article. Accessed 21 July 2019.

4   George Wagner, 'The Lair of the Bachelor', in Debra Coleman, Elizabeth Danze and Carol Henderson (eds), *Architecture and Feminism* (New York: Princeton Architectural Press, 1996), p.184.

5   Harriet Harriss, 'Goodbye Mister Bond: 007's Critical Advocacy for Feminism and Modernism', AAE, 2016 *Research Based Education*, vol.2, pp 348–57.

6   Tim Abrahams, 'Swedish Modern', *Blueprint*, no. 307, October 2011, p.65.

7   In 2013, *Newsweek* identified the Backus House as endangered. Up for sale, it was considered to be at risk from demolition due to its modest scale; Andrew Romano, 'Los Angeles's Endangered Modernist Homes', *Newsweek*, 16 August 2013. Available at https://www.newsweek.com/2013/08/16/los-angeless-endangered-modernist-homes-237842.html. Accessed 6 January 2020. The house was subsequently demolished in 2020. The original structure of the Nelson House remains intact; however, the interior is substantially altered, due to a lack of listing/preservation.

8   Beatriz Colomina, 'Outrage: Blindness to Women Turns Out to Be Blindness to Architecture Itself', *The Architectural Review*, 8 March 2018.

9   Álvarez and Gómez, op cit.

10   Oliver Wainright, 'Snubbed, Cheated, Erased: The Scandal of Architecture's Invisible Women', *The Guardian*, 16 October 2018. Available at https://www.theguardian.com/artanddesign/2018/oct/16/the-scandal-of-architecture-invisible-women-denise-scott-brown. Accessed 26 June 2020.

11   Richard Waite and Laura Mark, 'BBC Slammed for "Bias" after Patty Hopkins Is Sidelined in TV Show', *Architects' Journal*, 5 March 2014. Available at https://www.architectsjournal.co.uk/news/bbc-slammed-for-bias-after-patty-hopkins-is-sidelined-in-tv-show/8659720.article. Accessed 26 June 2020.

12   Jo Freeman, 'The Women's Liberation Movement: Its Origins, Structures and Ideas', Pittsburgh, KNOW, Inc., 1971, pp 8–9. Available at http://library.duke.edu/digitalcollections/wlmpc_wlmms01013/. Accessed 26 June 2020.

13   Álvarez and Gómez, op.cit.

14   Olivia Petter, 'More Than Half of Millennial Women Don't Identify as Feminist, Poll Finds', *The Independent*, 15 August 2018. Available at https://www.independent.co.uk/life-style/women/millennials-feminist-dont-identity-poll-refinery29-activism-a8492271.html. Accessed 21 July 2019.

15   Colomina, op.cit.

16   bell hooks, 'Choosing the Margin as a Space of Radical Openness', in *Yearning: Race, Gender and Cultural Politics* (Toronto: Between the Lines, 1990), pp 206–9.

17   Karen A. Franck, 'A Feminist Approach to Architecture: Acknowledging Women's Ways of Knowing', in Ellen Perry Berkeley and Matilda McQuaid (eds), *Architecture: A Place for Women* (Washington, DC: Smithsonian Institution Press, 1989).

Bibliography

BOOKS

Armstrong, Elizabeth (ed.), *Birth of the Cool: California Art, Design and Culture at Mid-century* (California: Orange County Museum of Art & Prestel Publishing, 2007)

Arwas, Victor, *Art Deco* (New York: Abrams Books, 1992)

Åselius, Gunnar, *The Rise and Fall of the Soviet Navy in the Baltic, 1921–1941* (Abingdon: Routledge, 2005)

Ashby, Charlotte, *Modernism in Scandinavia: Art, Architecture and Design* (London: Bloomsbury, 2017)

Banham, Reyner, *Los Angeles: The Architecture of Four Ecologies* (Oakland: University of California Press, 2009)

Benedict Brown, James, Harriet Harriss, Ruth Morrow and James Soane (eds), *A Gendered Profession: The Question of Representation in Space Making* (London: RIBA Books, 2016)

Bhambra, Gurminder K., Kerem Nişancıoğlu and Dalia Gebrial (eds), *Decolonising the University* (London: Pluto Press, 2018)

Brand, Stewart, *How Buildings Learn: What Happens After They're Built* (New York: Viking, 1994)

Brooks Pfeiffer, Bruce and Frank Lloyd Wright, *Treasures of Taliesin: Seventy-seven Unbuilt Designs* (Portland: Pomegranate, 1999)

Brooks Pfeiffer, Bruce and Frank Lloyd Wright, *Frank Lloyd Wright, 1867–1959: Building for Democracy* (Cologne: Taschen, 2004)

Brunnström, Lasse, *Swedish Design: A History* (London: Bloomsbury, 2018)

Codrington, Andrea, *Greta Magnusson Grossman – A Car and Some Shorts: One Architect's Journey from Sweden to Southern California* (Stockholm: Arkitekturmuseet, 2010)

Coleman, Debra, Elizabeth Danze and Carol Henderson (eds), *Architecture and Feminism* (New York: Princeton Architectural Press, 1996)

Conrads, Ulrich (ed.), *Programs and Manifestoes on 20th-Century Architecture*, trans. Michael Bullock (London: Lund Humphries, 1970)

Dines, Gail, Bob Jensen and Ann Russo, *Pornography: The Production and Consumption of Inequality* (Abingdon: Routledge, 2013)

Eckbo, Garrett, *Landscape for Living* (Amherst, MA: University of Massachusetts Press, 1950)

Eichler, Edward P., *Race and Housing: An Interview with Edward P. Eichler, President, Eichler Homes Inc.* (Santa Barbara: Fund for the Republic, 1964)

Englund, Magnus and Chrystina Schmidt, *Scandinavian Modern* (London: Ryland Peters & Small, 2007)

Espegel, Carmen, *Women Architects in the Modern Movement* (Abingdon: Routledge, 2018)

Friedman, Alice T., *Women and the Making of the Modern House* (New York: Harry N. Abrams Inc., 1998)

Greenhalgh, Paul, *Modernism in Design* (London: Reaktion Books, 1990)

Halén, Widar and Kerstin Wickman (eds), *Scandinavian Design Beyond the Myth: Fifty Years of Scandinavian Design from the Nordic Countries* (Stockholm: Arvinius, 2003)

Hall Kaplan, Sam and Julius Shulman, *LA Lost & Found: An Architectural History of Los Angeles* (Santa Monica, CA: Hennessey and Ingalls, 2000)

Harris, Frank and Weston David Bonenberger, *A Guide to Contemporary Architecture in Southern California* (Los Angeles: Watling, 1951)

Kane, Lily, *Greta Magnusson Grossman: Designer* (New York: R Gallery, 2000)

Kaplan, Wendy (ed.), *California Design, 1930–1965: Living in a Modern Way* (Cambridge, MA: MIT Press and Los Angeles County Museum of Art, 2011)

Lupton, Ellen, *Mechanical Brides: Women and Machines from Home to Office* (New York: Cooper-Hewitt, National Museum of Design, Smithsonian Institution; Princeton, NJ: Princeton Architectural Press, 1993)

Mattsson, Helena, Joan Ockman, Reinhold Martin, Penny Sparke and Sven-Olov Wallenstein (eds), *Swedish Modernism: Architecture, Consumption, and the Welfare State* (London: Black Dog Publishing, 2010)

Murphy, Keith M., Swedish Design: An Ethnography (Ithaca, NY: Cornell University Press, 2015)

Rice, Charles, *The Emergence of the Interior: Architecture, Modernity, Domesticity* (Abingdon: Routledge, 2007)

Soja, Edward W., *Thirdspace: Journeys to Los Angeles and Other Real-and-Imagined Places* (Oxford: Basil Blackwell, 1996)

Sparke, Penny, *The Modern Interior* (London: Reaktion Books, 2008)

Widenheim, Cecilia (ed.), *Utopia and Reality: Modernity in Sweden 1900–1960* (New Haven and London: Yale University Press, 2002)

CHAPTERS IN BOOKS

Åberg Waern, Karin, 'Modern Living', in Andrea Codrington, *Greta Magnusson Grossman – A Car and Some Shorts: One Architect's Journey from Sweden to Southern California* (Stockholm: Arkitekturmuseet, 2010)

Frampton, Kenneth, 'The Untimely Timeliness of Swedish Modernism', in Lucy Creagh, Helena Kåberg and Barbara Miller Lane (eds), *Modern Swedish Design: Three Founding Texts* (New York: Museum of Modern Art, 2008)

Franck, Karen A., 'A Feminist Approach to Architecture: Acknowledging Women's Ways of Knowing', in Ellen Perry Berkeley and Matilda McQuaid (eds), *Architecture: A Place for Women* (Washington, DC: Smithsonian Institution Press, 1989)

Harriss, Harriet and Naomi House, 'Interiority Complex', in James Benedict Brown, Harriet Harriss, Ruth Morrow and James Soane (eds), *A Gendered Profession: The Question of Representation in Space Making* (London: RIBA Books, 2016)

hooks, bell, 'Choosing the Margin as a Space of Radical Openness', in *Yearning: Race, Gender and Cultural Politics* (Toronto: Between the Lines, 1990)

McLeod, Mary, 'Everyday and "Other" Spaces', in Debra Coleman, Elizabeth Danze and Carol Henderson (eds), *Architecture and Feminism* (New York: Princeton Architectural Press, 1996)

Morrison, Arnault, 'A Typology of Places in the Knowledge Economy: Towards the Fourth Place', in Francesco Calabrò, Lucia Della Spina and Carmelina Bevilacqua (eds), *New Metropolitan Perspectives, Smart Innovation, Systems and Technologies*, vol.100 (Cham: Springer, 2018)

Naylor, Gillian, 'Swedish Grace . . . or the Acceptable Face of Modernism?', in Paul Greenhalgh (ed.), *Modernism in Design* (London: Reaktion Books, 1990)

Robach, Cilla, 'Design for Modern People', in Cecilia Widenheim (ed.), *Utopia and Reality: Modernity in Sweden 1900–1960* (New Haven and London: Yale University Press, 2002)

Rudberg, Eva, 'Utopia of the Everyday', in Cecilia Widenheim (ed.), *Utopia and Reality: Modernity in Sweden 1900–1960* (New Haven and London: Yale University Press, 2002)

Smith, Elizabeth A.T., 'Domestic Cool: Modern Architecture and its Image in Southern California', in Elizabeth Armstrong (ed.), *Birth of the Cool: California Art, Design and Culture at Mid-century* (California: Orange County Museum of Art and Prestel Publishing, 2007)

Sparke, Penny, 'The Designed Interior', in *The Modern Interior* (London: Reaktion Books, 2008)

Storgaard, Eva, 'Curating the Collective House: The Popularisation of a New Housing Model in 1930s Sweden', in Gaia Caramellino and Stéphanie Dadour (eds), *The Housing Project: Discourse, Ideals, Models and Politics in 20th Century Exhibitions* (Leuven: Leuven University Press, 2020)

Wagner, George, 'The Lair of the Bachelor', in Debra Coleman, Elizabeth Danze and Carol Henderson (eds), *Architecture and Feminism* (New York: Princeton Architectural Press, 1996)

JOURNAL ARTICLES

Abrahams, Tim, 'Swedish Modern', *Blueprint*, no.307, October 2011, pp 64–8

Álvarez, Eva and Carlo Gómez, 'The Invisible Women: How Female Architects Were Erased from History', *The Architectural Review*, 8 March 2017. Available at https://www.architectural-review.com/essays/the-invisible-women-how-female-architects-were-erased-from-history/10017481.article

'Magnusson Grossman', *American Artist*, vol.15, no.150, December 1951, pp 54–7

'New Furniture by Greta Grossman for Barker Brothers', *Arts & Architecture*, no.7, July 1947, p.32. Available at http://www.artsandarchitecture.com/issues/pdf01/1947_07.pdf

Barracano Schmidt, Dolores, 'The Great American Bitch', *College English*, vol.32, no.8, 1971, p.900

Björkman, Gunvor, 'Hos fru arkitekten', *Svenska Hem*, 1937, pp 183–8

Bullock, Nicholas, 'Review of *The Stockholm Exhibition 1930: Modernism's Breakthrough in Swedish Architecture* by Eva Rudberg', *Architectural Research Quarterly*, vol.4, no.1, March 2000, p.90. Available at https://www.cambridge.org/core/journals/arq-architectural-research-quarterly/article/stockholm-exhibition-1930-modernisms-breakthrough-in-swedish-architecture-by-eva-rudberg-stockholmia-forlag-stockholm-1999238-pp-c190-mono-and-c65-colour-illus-isbn-9170310912-price-sek-352/DCB86AC0BB9588B5614159D1EF97B4C7#

Byng, Malaika, 'Greta Magnusson Grossman retrospective, Stockholm', *Wallpaper**, 26 March 2010. Available at https://www.wallpaper.com/design/greta-magnusson-grossman-retrospective-stockholm

Cerio, G., 'Collecting: On the Rise. Designs by Ado Chale, Philippe Hiquily, and Greta Magnusson Grossman Take Off', *Architectural Digest*, vol.69, no.11, 1 November 2012, pp 79–83

Colomina, Beatriz, 'Outrage: Blindness to Women Turns Out to Be Blindness to Architecture Itself', *The Architectural Review*, 8 March 2018

Cuff, Dana, 'Review: *California Design, 1930–1965: Living in a Modern Way*', *Journal of the Society of Architectural Historians*, vol.72, no.1, March 2013, pp 100–101. Available at https://www.jstor.org/stable/10.1525/jsah.2013.72.1.100?seq=1#metadata_info_tab_contents

Danziger, Pamela, 'Ikea Realizes Democratic Design for the Home', *Forbes*, 12 June 2018. Available at https://www.forbes.com/sites/pamdanziger/2018/06/12/ikea-realizes-democratic-design-for-the-home/#4e1433f1469e

'Swedish Modern', *Designs* (Rehearsal Issue), August 1947

Exhibition review: 'Leonor Antunes: The Frisson of the Togetherness', *Domus*, 12 October 2017. Available at https://www.domusweb.it/en/art/2017/10/12/leonor-antunes-the-frisson-of-the-togetherness.html

Flinn, Andrew, 'Archival Activism: Independent and Community-led Archives, Radical Public History and the Heritage Professions', *InterActions: UCLA Journal of Education and Information Studies*, vol.7, no.2, 2011. Available at http://escholarship.org/uc/item/9pt2490x

Givens, Jean A., 'Review of Lucy Creagh, Helena Kåberg and Barbara Miller Lane (eds), *Modern Swedish Design: Three Founding Texts*', *CAA Reviews*, 25 November 2009. Available at http://www.caareviews.org/reviews/1357#.XLYWF2RKgfE

Gordon, Dan, '1900-talets Svenska formgivare: Axel Einar Hjort', *Sköna Hem*, no.11, October/November 2006

Griffith Winton, Alexandra, '"A Man's House Is his Art": The Walker Art Center's *Idea House* Project and the Marketing of Domestic Design 1941–1947', *Journal of Design History*, vol.17, no.4, 2004

Harper, Phineas, 'The Vision of the Home as a Tranquil Respite from Labour Is a Patriarchal Fantasy', *Dezeen*, 18 April 2019. Available at https://www.dezeen.com/2019/04/18/nuclear-family-home-tool-repression-phineas-harper/?utm_medium=email&utm_campaign=Daily%20Dezeen&utm_content=Daily%20Dezeen+CID_077e49a9ee188e47042f3f8c479374f6&utm_source=Dezeen%20Mail&utm_term=The%20vision%20of%20the%20home%20as%20a%20tranquil%20respite%20from%20labour%20is%20a%20patriarchal%20fantasy

Harriss, Harriet, 'Goodbye Mister Bond: 007's Critical Advocacy for Feminism and Modernism', AAE, 2016 *Research Based Education*, vol.2, pp 348–57

Havenhand, Lucinda Kaukas, 'A View from the Margin: Interior Design', *Design Issues*, vol.20, no.4, pp 32–42

Hedqvist, Hedvig, Exhibition review: 'Att minnas Greta Grossman', *Arkitektur*, vol.110, no.3, April 2010, pp 14–15

Kirkham, Pat, 'Humanizing Modernism: The Crafts, "Functioning Decoration" and the Eameses', *Journal of Design History*, vol.11, no.1, 'Craft, Modernism and Modernity', 1998, pp 15–29

Kvint, Annica, 'Greta Magnusson Grossman. på Arkitekturmuseet, Stockholm', *Nyheter*, 17 February 2010. Available at https://www.dn.se/kultur-noje/konstrecensioner/greta-magnusson-grossman-pa-arkitekturmuseet-stockholm/

Lawrence, Alexa, 'Leonor Antunes Channels 20th-century Designers and Artists in her Latest Work', *Architectural Digest*, 31 May 2015. Available at https://www.architecturaldigest.com/story/leonor-antunes-new-museum-new-york

Leary, Erin, '"The Total Absence of Foreign Subjects": The Racial Politics of US Interwar Exhibitions of Scandinavian Design', *Design and Culture*, vol.7, no.3, 2015, pp 283–312

Lees-Maffei, Grace, 'Introduction: Professionalization as a Focus in Interior Design History', *Journal of Design History*, vol.21, no.1, Spring 2008, pp 1–18. Available at https://doi.org/10.1093/jdh/epn007

Levine, Robert, 'Modern Architecture and Ideology: Modernism as a Political Tool in Sweden and the Soviet Union', *Momentum*, vol.5, no.1, University of Pennsylvania, 19 April 2018

Lustig, Alvin, 'Californian Modern', *Designs*, October 1947, pp 7–10

Maldonado-Torres, Nelson, 'Thinking through the Decolonial Turn: Post-continental Interventions in Theory, Philosophy, and Critique – An Introduction', *Transmodernity: Journal of Peripheral Cultural Production of the Luso-Hispanic World*, vol.1, no.2, 2011

'Milan Furniture Fair', *Icon*, no. 095, May 2011, pp 84–90

Mohanty, Chandra Talpade, 'Transnational Feminist Crossings: On Neoliberalism and Radical Critique', *Signs: Journal of Women in Culture and Society*, vol.38, no.4, 2013, pp 967–91

Näsström, Gustaf, 'Svensk heminredning i U.S.A', *Form*, 1943, p.188

Olausson, Magnus, 'Women Pioneers: Swedish Design in Between the Wars', *Art Bulletin of Nationalmuseum Stockholm*, vol.22, 2015, pp 163–6. Available at http://www.diva-portal.org/smash/get/diva2:998770/FULLTEXT02

Pehrson, Elsa, 'West Coast Designer', *American Swedish Monthly*, October 1944

'Single Storey House on a Very Steep Site, for Two People, Beverly Hills; Architect: Greta Grossman', *Progressive Architecture*, November 1957, pp 136–9

Runyan, Anne Sisson, 'Decolonizing Knowledges in Feminist World Politics', *International Feminist Journal of Politics*, vol.20, no.1, 2018, pp 3–8. Available at https://www.tandfonline.com/doi/full/10.1080/14616742.2018.1414403

Schioldager, Arianna, 'Greta Magnusson Grossman: Walking Away', *Art Papers*, vol.37, no.2, 2013, pp 36–41

Scott Brown, Denise, 'Room at the Top: Sexism and the Star System in Architecture', *Architectural Design*, vol.60, nos 1–2 (1990)

Waite, Richard and Laura Mark, 'BBC Slammed for "Bias" after Patty Hopkins Is Sidelined in TV Show',

Architects' Journal, 5 March 2014. Available at https://www.architectsjournal.co.uk/news/bbc-slammed-for-bias-after-patty-hopkins-is-sidelined-in-tv-show/8659720.article

NEWSPAPER AND MAGAZINE ARTICLES

Richards, Katie, 'Ikea's Top Designer on the Gift of Failure and the Future of Democratic Design: Marcus Engman Says Ikea is More than Just a Brand', *Adweek*, 25 May 2017. Available at https://www.adweek.com/creativity/ikeas-top-designer-on-thegift-of-failure-and-the-future-of-democratic-design/

'Fårskinnsmatta I vardagsrum: roliga hemidéer i Galerie Moderne', *Aftonbladet*, 9 May 1938

'Möbelkvinna öppnar funkisbutik', *Aftonbladet*, 3 April 1933

'Svenskt vardagsrum uppmärksammas på kontinenten', *Aftonbladet*, 13 September 1935

'Mat och mycket mat och mat I rättan tid', *Alla Kvinnors Flitiga Händer*, no.15, 1940

Henderson, Rose, 'A Swedish Furniture Designer in America: An Interview with Greta Magnusson Grossman', *American Artist*, no.150, December 1951

Langar, Suneet Zishan, '9 Incredibly Famous Architects Who Didn't Possess an Architecture Degree', *ArchDaily*, 19 June 2017. Available at https://www.archdaily.com/873850/9-incredibly-famous-architects-who-didnt-possess-an-architecture-degree

Reeder, Bettye, *Beverly Hills Citizen*, December 1941

Petre, Karin, 'Funktionalism och färg', *Boet*, October 1934, pp 190–94

'Greta Magnusson Grossman på Arkitekturmuseet, Stockholm', *Dagens Nyheter*, 17 February 2010. Available at https://www.dn.se/kultur-noje/konstrecensioner/greta-magnusson-grossman-pa-arkitekturmuseet-stockholm/

'Just nu . . .', *Dagens Nyheter*, 12 September 1951

'Vernissageronden', *Dagens Nyheter*, 14 February 1937

Warren, Tamara, Review: 'Greta Magnusson Grossman – A Car and Some Shorts', *Forbes*, 31 May 2011. Available at https://www.forbes.com/sites/tamarawarren/2011/05/31/greta-magnusson-grossman-a-car-and-some-shorts/#4b90efa395c2

'Exklusivt konsthantverk på Röhsska museet', *Göteborgs Morgonpost*, no.212, 12 September 1935

Wainright, Oliver, 'Snubbed, Cheated, Erased: The Scandal of Architecture's Invisible Women', *The Guardian*, 16 October 2018. Available at https://www.theguardian.com/artanddesign/2018/oct/16/thescandal-of-architecture-invisible-women-denise-scott-brown

'Up and Coming: Five Whose Stars are Shining in the Design World', *House & Garden*, June 1947, pp 30–39

Gordon, Elizabeth, 'The New American Look', *House Beautiful*, March, 1949

'Some Modern Is Nothing but Unpretentiousness', *House Beautiful*, March 1943

'Hos Sveriges enda kvinnliga möbelarkitekt', *Hvar 8 Dag*, 17 September 1933

Petter, Olivia, 'More Than Half of Millennial Women Don't Identify as Feminist, Poll Finds', *The Independent*, 15 August 2018. Available at https://www.independent.co.uk/life-style/women/millennials-feminist-dont-identity-poll-refinery29-activism-a8492271.html

Brown, Helen Weigel, 'Famed Artisans Create Beauty for Southland Homes', *Los Angeles Times*, 23 March 1941

'Home Furnishing Art Ranks High in Sweden', *Los Angeles Times*, 24 September 1941

Keeps, David A., 'Thinking Around the Box', *Los Angeles Times*, 7 February 2009. Available at https://www.latimes.com/archives/la-xpm-2009-feb-07-hm-grossman7-story.html

Krenzer, Jean, 'New Directions', *Los Angeles Times*, 5 June 1960

McHendrie, Janet, 'Smart Ways to Save Space', *Los Angeles Times*, 17 July 1949

Miller, Arthur, 'Art Parade Reviewed', *Los Angeles Times*, 9 March 1941

'Partitions for a Flexible House', *Los Angeles Times Sunday Magazine*, 11 August 1957

Romano, Andrew, 'Los Angeles's Endangered Modernist Homes', *Newsweek*, 16 August 2013

Schallert, Elza, 'A Noted Architect Speaks – Simplicity in Home Design Called Keynote to Family Preservation', *Los Angeles Times*, 8 July 1954

Alden Jewell, Edward, 'Swedish Art National in Effect', *New York Times*, 8 June 1930

'Kvinnlig möbelarkitekt, en av de första pa Skansen', *Nya Dagligt Allehanda*, 9 March 1933, p.9

Magnusson Grossman, Greta, 'Moderna hem i München och Wien', *Nya Dagligt Allehanda*, 28 July 1934

'Modern möbleringskonst har slagit igenom i hela Europa', *Nya Dagligt Allehanda*, 2 August 1934

Playboy, 1953, no.1, p.16

Wylie, Phillip, 'The Womanization of America', *Playboy*, 1958, p.78

'Swedish Designer to Work on West Coast', *Retailing*, 4 November 1940

'Acres of Modern Opened at Barker Bros., Los Angeles', *Retailing Home Furnishings*, 8 May 1947

'New Career Sought: Couple Arrive from Sweden', *San Francisco Examiner*, 27 July 1940

'Veckans vernissager', *Svenska Dagbladet*, 12 May 1935

'Retail Trade: The Los Angeles Spirit', *Time*, 1 January 1945. Available at http://content.time.com/time/magazine/article/0,9171,791859,00.html

'Barker Brother's Remodels Modern Floor', *Upholstering*, November 1947

'Arkitekter borde gå i hushållsskola', *Vårt Hem*, no. 1, 1935

'Hemma hos en kvinnlig möbleringsexpert', *Vecko Revyn*, no.10, 1936

'Good Design Is Appearance Plus Comfort: Swedish-born Designer Works Toward the Perfect Combination', *Western Upholstery Furniture & Bedding*, April 1953

BROCHURES

Hamlin, Talbot F., *Pencil Points*, June 1939, as quoted in *Sweden at the New York World's Fair* brochure, 1939, unpaginated

Mumford, Lewis, *New Yorker,* 17 June 1939, as quoted in *Sweden at the New York World's Fair* brochure, 1939, unpaginated

EXHIBITION CATALOGUES

Gheith, Jenny, *New Work: Leonor Antunes Brochure*, San Francisco Museum of Modern Art, 2016

Good Design, Museum of Modern Art, New York, 1952

Noyes, Eliot, *Organic Design in Home Furnishings*, MoMA, 1941. Available at https://www.moma.org/calendar/exhibitions/1803

Stavenow, Åke, Matis Hörlén, Åke H. Huldt and Elias Svedberg (eds), *Swedish Arts and Crafts: Swedish Modern: A Movement Towards Sanity in Design*, The Royal Swedish Commission for the New York World's Fair, New York, 1939

INTERVIEWS

Alton, Ebba, interview with Sigrid Eklund, 1987

Bohlin, Anne-Marie, interview with Karin Åberg Waern, 24 May 2009

Gubi, Jacob, interview with Harriet Harriss, 21 August 2018

Magnusson Grossman, Greta, interview with Sigrid Eklund, c.1988

ARCHIVES AND DATABASES

'A Brief History of the Work Home', *WorkHome* website. Available at http://www.theworkhome.com/history-workhome/

'Architects: Greta Grossman', *Pacific Coast Architecture Database.* Available at http://pcad.lib.washington.edu/person/274/

Carson, Jen, 'A Brief History of the Iconic Bungalows of LA', *LAist*, 15 April, 2016. Available at https://laist.com/2016/04/15/bungalow_history.php

Freeman, Jo, 'The Women's Liberation Movement: Its Origins, Structures and Ideas', Pittsburgh, KNOW, Inc., 1971, pp 8–9. Available at http://library.duke.edu/digitalcollections/wlmpc_wlmms01013/

'Greta Magnusson Grossman' page, *Design Within Reach* website. Available at https://www.dwr.com/search?q=Greta+Magnusson+Grossman&search-button=&lang=en_US

'Greta Magnusson Grossman' page, Los Angeles Conservancy website. Available at https://www.laconservancy.org/architects/greta-grossman

'Greta Magnusson Grossman' page, *Modern San Diego* website. Available at https://www.modernsandiego.com/people/greta-grossman

'Greta Magnusson Grossman: A Biography', *R & Company* website. Available at http://www.r-and-company.com/designers/greta-magnusson-grossman/

'Greta Magnusson Grossman' page, *Wikipedia* website. Available at https://en.wikipedia.org/wiki/Greta_Magnusson-Grossman

'Hill Houses 1920–1955', *Los Angeles Historic Resources Survey*

Ikea, 'About' page. Available at https://www.ikea.com/ms/en_AU/about_ikea/the_ikea_way/history/1940_1950.html

Krondahl, Hans, 'Tema Lunning Prize Winners', *Runeberg*. Retrieved 3 January 2018. Also see http://danishdesignreview.com/the-lunning-prize

Lambert, Susan, *Greta Magnusson Grossman: Furniture and Lighting*, The Drawing Center, New York, 1984. Available at https://issuu.com/drawingcenter/docs/drawingpapers81_grossman

Torre, Susana, 'Feminism and Architecture, Part 1: Feminist Contributions', 21 August 2014. Available at https://archiparlour.org/feminism-and-architecture-part-1-the-contribution-of-feminism/

EVENTS

Getting Going for Greta Magnusson Grossman, SAH/SCC Talk & Tour, Saturday 9 February 2013, Society of Architectural Historians: Southern California Chapter. Available at http://www.sahscc.org/site/index.php?function=past_event_details&id=136

RADIO

Dufva, Anneli, 'Formgivaren Greta Magnusson: framgångsrik men okänd', *Sveriges Radio*, 18 February 2010. Available at https://sverigesradio.se/sida/artikel.aspx?programid=478&artikel=3449595

THESES

Busang, Alexandra, *Architectural Consumption in Los Angeles: Modernism, Power and the Aesthetic of Plenty*, MA thesis, 2015. Available at https://yorkspace.library.yorku.ca/xmlui/bitstream/handle/10315/30022/Busgang_Alexandra_R_2015_Masters.pdf?sequence=2&isAllowed=y

Nelson, Nona, *The Influence of Swedish, Finnish and Danish Textiles on Contemporary American Fabrics*, MSc, unpublished thesis, 1957

Index

Note: *italic* page numbers indicate figures; page numbers followed by n. indicate notes; Greta Magnusson Grossman is abbreviated to GMG in headings and subheadings.

Illustration Credits

Some images were originally in colour but have been converted to greyscale for this book. The reproduction of the illustrations listed below (by Figure/Plate number) is courtesy of the following copyright holders:

Almberg and Preinitz (courtesy of the Greta Magnusson Grossman design records and papers located at R & Company, New York) 30; Plate 3

Ateljé Uggla (courtesy of the Greta Magnusson Grossman design records and papers located at R & Company, New York) 31

Bergne Reklamfoto (courtesy of the Greta Magnusson Grossman design records and papers located at R & Company, New York) Plate 1

Daniel Funk (image courtesy of Leonor Antunes and SFMoMA, San Francisco) 35, 36

Donald J. Higgins (courtesy of the Greta Magnusson Grossman design records and papers located at R & Company, New York) 32, 37, 44, 46; Plate 9, Plate 10

Edward Stojakovic 29

flickr (https://www.flickr.com/photos/benledbetter-architect/5577053724) 38

flickr (https://www.flickr.com/photos/chs_commons/15301961647) 26

Fredric Boukari 39, 40, 41, 42, 43

Greta Magnusson Grossman design records and papers located at R & Company, New York Foreword, 2, 3, 10, 11, 12, 13, 14, 15, 16, 17, 18, 19, 20, 25, 34, 45; Plate 2, Plate 6

G.W. Cronquist (https://www.flickr.com/photos/tekniskamuseet/7795226356) 4

Harry H. Baskerville, Jr (courtesy of the Greta Magnusson Grossman design records and papers located at R & Company, New York) Plate 4

Holger.Ellgaard (https://commons.wikimedia.org/wiki/File:Stockholms_stadsbibliotek_2010.jpg) 6

Joe Kramm (courtesy of R & Company, New York) Plate 20

John Hartley (courtesy of the Greta Magnusson Grossman design records and papers located at R & Company, New York) 47, 48; Plate 11, Plate 12, Plate 13, Plate 14, Plate 15, Plate 16

Julius Schulman (courtesy of the Greta Magnusson Grossman design records and papers located at R & Company, New York) 1, 23, 24, 28, 33; Plate 7, Plate 8

Maynard L. Parker (courtesy of the Greta Magnusson Grossman design records and papers located at R & Company, New York) 21; Plate 5

R & Company, New York 22; Plate 17, Plate 18, Plate 19, Plate 21

Swedish National Heritage Board @ Flickr Commons 5

TL Stockholm Sweden 9

Wikimedia Commons (https://commons.wikimedia.org/wiki/File:Stockh_1930_Paradiset.jpg) 8

Wikimedia Commons (https://commons.wikimedia.org/wiki/File:Frankfurterkueche.jpg) 27

Wikimedia Commons (https://commons.wikimedia.org/wiki/File:Pavillon_L%27Esprit_Nouveau.jpg) 7

Yara Feghali and Viviane El Kmati 50, 51, 52, 53, 54, 55, 56, 57, 58, 59, 60

Zoe Beloff 49